Moving
UP

Moving UP

Ten Steps to
Turning Your Life Around
and Getting to the Top!

Suzan Johnson Cook

DOUBLEDAY

New York   London   Toronto   Sydney   Auckland

PUBLISHED BY DOUBLEDAY

Copyright © 2008 by Suzan D. Johnson Cook

Published in the United States by Doubleday, an imprint of The Doubleday Broadway Publishing Group, a division of Random House, Inc., New York.
www.doubleday.com

DOUBLEDAY and the portrayal of an anchor with a dolphin are registered trademarks of Random House, Inc.

Book design by Nicola Ferguson

LIBRARY OF CONGRESS CATALOGING-IN-PUBLICATION DATA
Johnson Cook, Suzan D. (Suzan Denise), 1957–
    Moving up : ten steps to turning your life around and getting to the top! / Suzan Johnson Cook. — 1st ed.
            p.   cm.
    Includes bibliographical references.
    (alk. paper)
1.   Success—Religious aspects—Christianity.   I.   Title.
    BV4598.3.J64 2008
    248.4—dc22
2007049460

ISBN 978-0-385-52429-2

PRINTED IN THE UNITED STATES OF AMERICA

10 9 8 7 6 5 4 3 2 1

First Edition

This book is dedicated to all those who are ready to move up,
to Adele Bond, Mercedes Nesfield, Alexis Revis Yeoman,
Gail Harris, Theresa Harrison, and Bertha Williams,
who keep me up, and in loving memory of Yolanda Denise King,
who moved up to Higher Ground.

Contents

—

Acknowledgments

"Word **UP!**" is a familiar twenty-first-century saying among teens intended to get the attention of those who need to listen and be lifted up. This book about moving up will capture your attention and advance you toward a new spirit of liberty and "UPness." I share from a moving biblical story the tips and steps to a brand-new you. Remember, life is a journey, a series of significant steps one takes. At times, they are forward, sometimes backward, but always important. These steps I am sharing with you ascend upward toward a staircase pointing toward Standing up, Speaking up, Looking up, Booking up, Kissing up, Listening up, Hanging up, Making up, Waking up, and Cheering up.

Some of those who've helped me stay up and pray up were those responsible for this book. Trace Murphy, my editor, and the entire Doubleday/Random House team; Lois de la Haba, my literary agent, who not only hooks me up but also "books me up" and introduces me to heaven-sent writers like Larry Keefauver and wonderful publishers like Doubleday.

Thank you, Larry, for helping my voice speak up and come out in this book.

I must also speak up and give a shout out to my husband, Ron, and sons, Christopher and Samuel, who share my life, love, and legacy, and who give me room to write, dream, pray, and have my EBs when I need them. EBs are affection my sons give to me when they think I'm "emotionally breaking-down." As you "move up" in life, remember that Mommy loves you.

To my BCF Church family, Wonderful Wall Street™ Wednesdays, and Womens' Ministry International, who allowed me to share these ups in oral form before they were even written, and to Capt. Gail Harris, who said, "That's your next book right there." You were right.

Moving
UP

Introduction

Stuck? Start

Moving Up! --------------------------------

In the man's world of Old Testament patriarchal society, some five generations of sons after Jacob, the begetting of boys came to a screeching halt with the birth of five daughters to Zelophehad—Mahlah, Noah, Hoglah, Milcah, and Tirzah. A son and father without a son, Zelophehad had no male heir to receive his inheritance.

> In ancient Israel the property of a deceased person was usually distributed according to law or tribal custom. Written wills were rarely used. The real and personal property of a father was normally divided among his sons. A larger amount, usually a double portion, went to the eldest son, who assumed the care of his mother and unmarried sisters.[1]

No sons available, no suffrage, women's rights, or civil rights law. What's a woman to do? Would the family legacy be transferred to an uncle by bypassing the rightful women heirs? Those sisters, even without a constituted voice, found their voice to move up into prominence instead of down into obscurity. The five collected themselves corporately as one and stood before the most imposing male figure their culture had ever seen—Moses.

Zelophehad was a dad, a son, and a grandson, but he had no son. The story takes place in a time when male patriarchy and dominance ruled—what men did, said, and wanted was all that mattered. Women were property whose primary worth was measured in the birthing and raising of children (particularly male heirs). They were to care for the home, but not own the house. When Zelophehad died having no son, the question that would have most probably resounded in the minds of male relatives was this: *Which man would receive the inheritance?*

That is, until some *sisters* came on the scene!

No man would advocate for them. All that the men had to go on was precedence. But the women had more going for them—they had upward-moving boldness rooted in a legacy of faithful loyalty. "Our father died in the wilderness, but he was not in the company of those who had gathered against the Lord," they declared. Their family lineage was just as worthwhile as that of their uncles. Their claim to a future was just as valid as anyone else's and they were willing to go up to Moses and ask for their rightful inheritance. They reached up to grasp their rightful inheritance and God "caused the inheritance of their father to pass to them" setting up a new precedent for future generations.[2]

These are the daughters of Zelophehad. They're not the names you normally hear when you think of famous women in the Bible. They're not Mary Magdalene and not Mary the mother of Jesus . . . not Ruth or Deborah and not Esther or Rahab, but rather Mahlah, Noah, Hoglah, Milcah, and Tirzah, five sisters who were united. United in going forward not backward, being blessed not cursed, seeking more than what's traditional, speaking up not staying quiet, moving up not staying down, they were . . .

Standing Up . . .

Speaking Up . . .

Looking Up . . .

Booking Up . . .

Kissing Up . . .

Listening Up . . .

Hanging Up . . .

Making Up . . .

Waking Up and Cheering Up.

It may not be clear to you now but as we explore their courage, boldness, and initiative, these sisters will become an inspiration and example for your life as they have been for mine and for countless other women and men through the centuries. You don't have to be a woman to look up to a woman. Anyone can learn how to be up from those who show the way.

In a time when women had little prominence, the daughters of Zelophehad came before one of the great leaders in history. They were not intimidated or cowering. Without guile, they were full of fiery conviction shaped in the crucible of being right. With the death of their father, instead of going down into grief and obscurity they went to the front of the line refusing to settle for less. For the first time, they rose up and they may well have framed the issue this way: Dad had a life, but now it's time for us to live. Where is what's due us? Give us the inheritance of our father? Don't we deserve what our Dad had?

A Kairos Moment

Eternity can invade time and space. Such intervention is called a *kairos* moment—in the Greek this word speaks of a certain, particular time or season, an appointed moment, an opportunity. We may call it a crisis, because we don't understand the times, but God often orchestrates these *kairos* moments so that He can reveal answers that we need for the critical questions in our lives. We could not foresee it, but God knew the *kairos* moment was coming. God divinely aligns *kairos* moments in history such as when the wise men were following the star in the east. They had been astrologists all their lives but those particular stars lined up in a way that questions were answered and a direction and a destiny for the future was revealed.

In this story of the daughters of Zelophehad, this particular set of circumstances—their father dying without male heirs—was a *kairos* moment creating the opportunity for them to stand up and speak up. They would either die figuratively and literally along with their father or they could stand *up* for the first time in their lives. They could rise *up* and become the women that God would have them to be. A favorite text of mine fits here: "They that wait upon the Lord shall mount up [rise up, move up] with wings of eagles."[3] They had waited patiently all of their lives for this *kairos* moment to rise up, not in their own strength but in God's. God lifts us up with power and strength to soar through the crises of transitory challenges.

There are so many crises recorded in history that were simply missed opportunities for people to go *up* to the next level in their lives and destinies. But for those of us with the courage, boldness, audacity, and passion to move up, such catalytic moments will catapult us into a new consciousness.

Remember Job? His greatest crisis came when he had wealth, cattle, and children to carry on his legacy, but they were all taken away. He said, "Though he slay me yet shall I trust him."[4] Job looked up to God. He stood up against his circumstances and bad-mouthing companions.

Remember Daniel, who was taken from his homeland and told not to pray? He had a crisis and he said, "Even though they tell me not to pray I cannot stop because that is my connection to my Creator."[5]

These sisters faced an economic crisis. All of their support would have been cut off had they not said what they did when they did. Martin Luther King Jr. said, "The ultimate measure of a man [or woman] is not where he stands in moments of comfort and convenience, but where [s]he stands at times of challenge and controversy."[6] This was their crisis, their father was gone, and they lived in a time and a town where men made the decisions. For the first time they, as daughters of Zelophehad, had to come to the forefront. I believe there are lessons in this story from these sisters, the daughters of Zelophehad, that will help those of us who want to go up with our own lives, make a difference, go over the top, and have impact in our *kairos* moments. You may be in or coming out of a *kairos* moment right now or just ready for a change that will take you over the top. That's how and why you found this book! Now declare with me, "I'm moving up."

I believe people are seeking answers and that's why we see in the movies and we read in all the tabloids about people seeking fulfillment. We read about people trying to find answers, just like those of you reading these pages of this book. Recently we learned of the unhappiness of Anna Nicole Smith who had many things materially but did not have some of the fulfillment that she so desperately needed. This is a story not just about material wealth and inheritance but about fulfillment and coming to the place in life where I believe God would have us to be.

So I entitled this book *Moving Up*. In the book I describe ten steps for moving up. Of course, there are more than ten steps. The list could be almost infinite, but this is a good start. I believe Zelophehad's daughters moved up and some wonderful things happened as a result. As you get to the end of the story you will see that they moved up. Where you start does not have to be where you end up. Even if you feel you're "at the bottom," there's no place to go but up! Declare with me, "I'm not moving out, I'm moving up. I'm not giving up, I'm moving up."

Up Moves You Through Life's Transitions

This is not just a story for women. This is a story for anyone who is facing a turning point in their life. For me this deals with a critical turning point. While writing this book, I hit the age of fifty, which is a transitional year. I now have more years behind me than in front of me. Just after the celebration of my fiftieth, one of my most dear friends just one year older than I died. So mortality and passion are all part of my thoughts right now. Not only do I ask what would Jesus do? I ask what do *I* want to do?

You may be facing significant transition in your life. Maybe it's a career move or a new location; maybe it's aging parents you must care for or growing children ready to leave the nest; maybe it's a relational change or a new direction in life. For both men and women this is a message that will help you to feel confident in terms of where you are and who you are as well as feel confident of the possibilities of God. Some call it "reinvention." I say it is an intentional declaration you make to "move up."

When you *look up*, you will be able to really say that with God "all things are possible." So, like the daughters of Zelophehad, you will realize you're not stuck where you are. Your past doesn't determine your future. Culture and tradition do not dictate your next move. Others can't keep you down when up is your decision and stuck isn't an option. A delay isn't a denial!

So this book is for all who want to go to a new place in their lives in the arenas of career, family, education, work, recreation, relationships, purpose, and meaning.

Are there times when you awaken in the middle of the night full of questions? Then you are in a transition. Sometimes it's in the middle of the day as you're sitting at your desk and you say, "I can't do this any more. I know it well, I've done this for many years but there is something more that I feel is coming to me."

If you're stuck or in transition . . . if you are down or have hit bottom . . . even if you're moving but not seeming to get anywhere, up is for you. This is the book that will take you to your new place. This is a book for people who want to change their down feelings and are determined to look up to God. I believe God is lining up all of the yeses in your life. You have had all the nos, but I believe there is a yes waiting with your name on it. This book is about moving up from where you are and becoming what God would have you be. A "no" is just one door closing on your way to your yes.

My children have been studying language. They have learned about words that sound like what they describe. It's called onomatopoeia and words like *fizz* or *ping-pong* or *up* suggest in their sound what they mean or do. *Up* has a lifting sound and suggests movement that is positive and filled with potential. When people are depressed, when people are feeling out of it, they look down. This is a book to help them look up.

First, *up* can be a physical movement. Looking at the

hills of Palestine, the shepherd and king, David, gave us an example, saying,

> *I look up to the mountains—*
> *does my help come from there?*
> *My help comes from the LORD,*
> *who made the heavens and the earth![7]*

Second, the upward move is *moving up* toward God. Jesus had a horizontal relationship with those He touched but He was also reaching up. He had a horizontal relationship when He touched people, but He was always moving up with His hand always stretched toward God.

Up is the movement and direction toward possibility—"with God nothing is impossible."[8] Up is the movement of reaching. Up is where we're going. When you watch birds take off, they don't fly down, they fly up. They leave the ground after they've found their food. They leave the place where they have come for their nurturing and their nourishment, and then they fly up, they soar. Moving up, you will begin to discover who you are. You may have felt you had clipped wings. This book will help you to begin to fly, moving up toward your God-given *kairos* moments filled with yeses and possibilities in life. Read on and start *moving up!*

CHAPTER 1

Stand Up! ----------------------------------

tand Up" is a command to yourself. You may sing songs that command yourself to do something. As a child, I sang, "O be careful little mouth what you say. . . ." What did you sing? What parent tapes echo in your memory commanding you to do or say certain things? Can you complete the thought, "Cleanliness is next to _____"?

All of our lives, we receive internal and external directives. Standing up declares that I have made a decision to change my posture, mentally and physically, to one of action. I've been staying in a position so long but now I'm ready to change it. Fannie Lou Hamer was known for the phrase, "I'm sick and tired of being sick and tired." There are things that happen for us when we change our posture.

Listen carefully. I hear a voice saying, *"Stand up, pick up your sleeping mat, and walk!"*[1] Imagine sitting around with a handicap for thirty-eight years expecting everyone else to do something for you . . . blaming everyone else for your lack of initiative, planning, or desire to be well. Such was the paralytic who was lying by the pool of Bethsaida. That's why Jesus, when He went by the man, said something like this, "You've got to stand up, take up your bed and walk. You have to change from the position that you have been in to one of action."

Oh, I hear your excuses. You were born that way. A relationship broke your heart. A promotion was not given to you. A terrible accident crippled you. Somebody hurt you. It wasn't your fault. What has happened to you may have been done by someone else. How you have responded was what you did to yourself.

Proverbs declares "As a man thinketh, so is he."[2] The mental, the physical position you place yourself in determines where you're going and how you'll go there. So a "stand up attitude" determines one's altitude. I want to go higher. My attitude determines my altitude. Say to yourself, "I'm tired of being at status quo, of being like this heart machine where the line is just going straight across. I want to see some action; I want to see some zig-zags on this monitor. I must get beyond a flat line! I must get beyond a flat life."

Stand Up and Be Noticed

The daughters of Zelophehad were not afraid to stand up. They had what my grandmother called spunk; they had what the Jewish grandmothers call chutzpah. They had to stand up for something right. I've heard it said, "You must stand for something or you will fall for anything." Cultural tradition went against them. Precedence was lacking for their actions. No women had done what they planned to do before. They could have sat in their tents and bemoaned their fate. Or, they could do something different. They could stand up. God took notice when they stood up. Sometimes you must stand up to be noticed!

A wonderful pleasure in my life has been meeting many women and men who were movers and shakers—life and history changers. One was my other mother, who just recently transitioned. Her name was Mrs. Coretta Scott King. Many of you know her from the Civil Rights movement. She was married to the late Rev. Dr. Martin Luther King Jr., one of the greatest civil rights leaders in history. She touched my life in a profound and incredible way. She was a woman who stood up against incredible odds. This woman had lynchings all around her; she had a bombing in her newborn baby's bedroom. She experienced disgusting acts of racism during America's Jim Crow era. She lived through all of that. But she always took the high road, she always held her head up and walked erect, and she always moved up in terms of taking the higher ground. No matter what people did to try to pull her down or how many times people would try to pull her away, she would always take the higher ground.

Coretta **stood up** for justice, she stood up for civil rights; that was her life's work. As a matter of fact she said, "It's not a matter of how long you live, it's a matter of how *well* you live." She stood up for things she believed in and we are all beneficiaries of her life's stance.

Are You Willing to Stand Up?

So what I'm saying now is it's time for you to determine what you are going to stand up for in your life. What are you going to stand up for? There's a song and a Bible passage that commands, "When you've done all you can, stand."[3]

There are other women and men in my life who have stood up for things that they believe in. We must each find those who are our heroes and she-roes and learn to stand up with them. See what they stood up for and begin to emulate their values. One of the great things that I do when I'm on the road is I look in those night tables and I begin to read the stories and biographies of the great men and women who stood up for something. I read of the hotel giants like Hilton, Marriott, and Helmsley as well as the publishing like Earl Graves and John Johnson, all of whom had to stand up in the midst of tremendous adversity. They may have had meager beginnings or meager means but they stood up for what they believed in. Standing up is about where your attitude lies and how you're going to begin to think as you go forward.

The Great Take a Stand Up!

Another woman who deeply influenced my life was Dr. Dorothy Height. As I write this, she is ninety-five years old. I recently celebrated her ninety-fifth birthday with her in New York City. She not only had racism but she had sexism to deal with in her life. She wanted to attend college and be a minister in a time when the odds against her were great. She applied and by phone she was accepted at Barnard College, but when she arrived there, they had a different story. But she stood up and courageously said, "I'm here, I'm here to get an education. I'm standing up for what my parents fought and died for." She went on to NYU and received her degree. Recently Barnard brought her back and granted her an honorary degree. When I became the first female president of a historically male leadership group, Dr. Height stood up with me as "one of the first," because she understood what this moment meant for me, and identified with what it took to be standing there. As we faced the twelve thousand leaders who had gathered there, she proclaimed, "This is a great moment. Dr. Johnson Cook is able to stand where I wanted to stand years ago."

Standing up takes courage. When you stand up it does not mean that things will not come against you to try to either crush your spirit or try to knock you back down. But standing up says, I have made a decision that my posture is going to change. Standing up is going from sitting to standing, sometimes from laying to standing. It's an attitude that says, I am going to be about something in this life. I have an assignment and I am standing for it. I am standing with God for it.

If you never stand up, you never risk falling or failing. John Maxwell writes about failing forward. In other words, when you risk standing, you may fail, but move forward anyway—don't go back. You will always learn something. Grow. Be strong and courageous. Don't allow fear to paralyze you. Stand up again. I stood alongside President Clinton in 1993, successful on my third attempt to become a White House Fellow—I had failed my way to success because I had stood up for what I knew was right and had the courage to speak up at the right time. I will talk about speaking up later in this book.

Standing up takes faith. Picture yourself as an inflatable boxing toy with a weighted base, a bop bag. Every time you hit that toy, it falls over, but it bounces right back up. Nothing can keep it down unless it's deflated. Refuse to decompress or deflate. When someone punches the breath out of you, inhale. Let God's spirit breathe new hope and life into you. Believe who He says you are, not what others say to defame and degrade you. You are a child of the King, bow to no negative circumstance or critical diatribe, stand up!

A story in Acts narrates how Paul comes across a crippled man in Lystra. "And seeing that he had faith to be healed, he [Paul] says to the man with a loud voice, stand up straight on your feet."[4] There's a miracle that happens because faith says to God, "I trust you and I believe that those things that you did for others you can also do for me and even more." You combine faith with your ability to stand and what happens is that healing comes.

In the Gospels, Jesus often taught standing up and noticed the faith of people and invited them to stand up and seize a miracle. He tapped into the power of faith already present within them. Many think we have to wait and tap into something outside of ourselves but really faith is already dormant in you and it's waiting to be activated. That's why Hebrews 11:1 begins with the words *"Now* faith." "Now" faith means I'm ready to stand up Now. There's a miracle that happens when you activate the faith inside of you and you connect with your Creator. It doesn't take much—faith the size of a tiny mustard seed can activate extraordinary power within you.

Healing comes in many forms. It's not just your physical healing but something happens for you emotionally and spiritually because God takes you from sitting in one place to standing up in a new place.

There's a miracle that happens when God sees that you have faith to be healed and that you are ready to activate that faith. It's a holy partnership when you and God get together, it's a majority. What God is doing here when femininity, or masculinity, and the divinity get together is releasing power. God is saying, "I have created you. You are fearfully and wonderfully made."[5] God is saying to you, "Now I am ready for you to take that which I have breathed into you, My very breath, and allow it to be activated in your life."

I Had to Stand Up . . . What About You?

I was one of the children born to the late Dorothy C. and Wilbert T. Johnson. They were rural southern, sharecroppers who had to work in the fields in this lifetime but they stood up. So I had an example of my parents standing up. My parents came out of the fields of the south and my mother went into education and became a teacher and got two master's degrees. Then she went back to the south and taught all of her cousins and nephews and nieces. Then she moved to New York and taught for twenty-two years in the New York City public school system and became a guidance counselor. I saw a woman stand who had no financial means whatsoever when she began, who had had nine brothers and sisters that all died before she was twelve years old. But before she died not only had she taught successfully as a teacher and guidance counselor, but she became an entrepreneur, opening a business in New York which employed many of the families she had empowered. She moved up.

So she grew up without siblings and parentless because of the great era of polio, tuberculosis, and what they used to call dropsy (elephantiasis). There were many infectious diseases that were just taking people out all around her, especially poor people. Health care was not available nor affordable. Poverty's aim is to keep you down, but faith's aim is to lift you up—up out of the circumstances which oppress you or hold you back. She ended up being a young woman who had to live going from house to house with cousins and aunts that would take her in. But she stood up and said, I'm getting out of these fields and I see education as my route out. She worked all the way through college. She could not join any sororities or anything like that because of the time in which she lived and her economic restraints. She worked as secretary to the college president and because of the determination in her life she came forth.

At the same time my father, who came from the rural south at the age of fifteen, worked and sent money back to all of his nieces and nephews, putting them all through college. He didn't finish high school himself but he put them all through college. Then at age forty-four he started his own family. I was born when he was fifty years old. Not because my father had other families but because my father said to himself, I have ability within me to get out of these fields and do something with my life. Like the daughters of Zelophehad said, "My dad died of honorable means." My mother and father met on their first day in New York City, fell in love, and began to build their life together.

So their standing up DNA was deposited into me when I was born into this family. I began to know what standing up really meant from the very start. It meant no matter what the odds, no matter what the beginning, no matter how adverse the situation, there is a power within you. "For with God, all things are possible." (St. Luke 1:37).

What was their fuel? They were people of faith. Faith fuels the will within you to stand up. Faith gives you stand-up-ability. We were in church and the church was in us. It was our faith community. In our church community we were taught this from the beginning. We would be sitting and singing the hymns with our parents at five and six years old and someone would lean over and say, "What college are you going to?" I'd say, "I'm just learning to read." But what they were doing was fortifying my faith and my strength and planting the seeds of strength by saying you can be anything you want.

Fast forwarding, my parents sent me to Riverdale Country School, a prestigious private school. In seventh grade they began to see that I had some gifts and talents that could have been lost in the public school system where we lived and in the street culture that awaited school children as they left school each day. I was one of two African American children in my class, not just in one class but the whole grade. By the ninth grade when student elections rolled around, there had never been a person of color at the head of a class before. There had not been many people of color in the school and the odds were totally against such an outcome. But it was at that moment that the climate was right and I had earned the respect and the congeniality of my classmates. I became the first African American to ever be head of all the junior high grades known as the "junior school" in the history of the school. I think that was a stand up moment in my life.

That experience fortified me to take a stand not just as a woman, but like the daughters of Zelophehad, also as a cultural minority. We must never diminish that. While I was head of the class, we began programs that would help the community to be culturally sensitive to all the different cultural groups that were in the school. We got to learn about one another and not be afraid of one another. I think for me that was a stand up moment, I had to stand up because I had to go against such great odds, but I believed in God and I believed in the God that was in me. That was an example of faith put into action and the results were there.

As an adult, I became a White House advisor to President Clinton. A pastor, a Baptist pastor, had never been a White House advisor before, so they were not sure where to put me once I went through the whole screening process and received that appointment. But I believed I was supposed to be in that place at that time. I believed that being in the White House was my assignment and that God had prepared me.

I remember walking in the front door of the White House and, as I reflected back on my parents, I said to myself, My goodness, I have moved from relatives who used an outhouse to the front door of the White House. What a moment that was. I can remember it like it was yesterday and that was twenty years ago. My stand up DNA took me forward and there was no turning back! Just this past year, former president Bill Clinton came to celebrate my birthday and ministry anniversary and listened to me minister. As I stood on the stage next to him, he remarked, "This is a woman who has courage and with whom I stand as a friend." What an honor!—to stand up WITH a president!

Stand Up People Exhibit Selfless Courage

Every up requires virtue—character qualities rooted deeply in the nature of God that are implanted within us as we are created in God's image. A virtue exhibits the very best in us and brings out the very best in others. What God deposited within us lies dormant until we risk trusting God to shape and mold us like a potter shaping clay. The prophet Jeremiah spoke of seeing a potter working on a clay jar:

> The LORD gave another message to Jeremiah. He said, "Go down to the shop where clay pots and jars are made. I will speak to you while you are there." So I did as he told me and found the potter working at his

wheel. But the jar he was making did not turn out as he had hoped, so the potter squashed the jar into a lump of clay and started again.[6]

As God shapes us through difficulties and trials, as difficult circumstances press in on us the way the pressure of the potter's hands mold the pot's shape, we discover what's within us. On the surface are various emotions and habitual responses that soon give way to either strength or weakness, courage or fear. The psalmist admonishes us, "Wait on the Lord; be of good courage, and He shall strengthen your heart. Wait, I say, on the Lord!"[7]

I discovered that my first emotional response to difficult people or situations often tempted me to take a wrong direction or overreact with a destructive action. Instead of courageously standing up, I would be tempted to react with my fight or flight instinct. It takes courage to stand up and wait. Waiting requires strength and boldness. Waiting may mean that we endure attacks, insults, pain, and grief. However, right overcomes might when that might is illegitimate and abusive power seeks to intimidate and manipulate us into a position that surrenders to evil out of fear.

Dietrich Bonhoeffer, the courageous Lutheran pastor who stood up to Hitler's Nazism and even helped plot to assassinate the Führer, found a courage and strength within himself that God had given him. Ultimately, his standing up cost him his life, as it has countless others who have stood up throughout the centuries like St. Paul, Joan of Arc, John Wycliffe, Martin Luther King Jr., and many other Christian martyrs who refused to bow to wrong.

Righteousness and justice. What fuels the strength and courage we need to stand up? Let me suggest that the virtue of courage begins with justice and righteousness. When your cause is just, stand up. When righteousness runs like a mighty stream, stand up.[8] When the innocent suffer and the weak are abused, stand up. If the poor cannot afford to take the next step up out of their poverty, stand up with your money and your commitment to empower them. When a child has no advocate, become one and stand up. You cannot keep silent; your silence stains your hands with innocent blood.

Standing up involves *right motive, right timing,* and *right action.* Too often people aggressively rush into a situation, taking a stand that is ill-timed and selfishly motivated. Examine yourself. Ask yourself these questions before you stand up:

- Are my motives pure and right?
- Do I have my facts right?
- Is the way I am taking my stand bringing honor to God and respecting the God-given rights of others?

- Is now the right time for a stand or should I wait on God's guidance for just the right moment?

It may seem that courage and patience are opposites but that's true only for people who are poorly informed or selfishly prompted to action. Doing the right thing at the wrong time hurts everyone involved. Fools rush in to take a stand only to lose everything for no purpose and no ultimate gain.

Standing up invokes selfless courage. Standing up may ultimately benefit self but it will always lift up others. Standing up may preserve one's rights and liberties in the long term, but it will always protect and defend the rights of others. In order to redeem humanity, Jesus stood up to the unjust and unrighteous leaders of His day. Such a stand looked foolish to the powerful and hopeless to the powerless, but ultimately the cross saved us and exalted Him. Bold and strong courage mark those who stand up, who are willing to risk everything including their fortunes and their lives for what is just and right. God speaks to the stand up person in the same way today as He did in ancient Israel. Hear this encouragement for yourself: "Have I not commanded you? Be strong and courageous. Do not be terrified; do not be discouraged, for the LORD your God will be with you wherever you go."[9]

What Will It Take for You?

Look around you. Is your focus on what has kept you down? Yes, everyone has trials, problems, and failures. They constitute an ugly quagmire, a quicksand of defeat sucking you into the pit of despair. As long as you wallow in your misery, you will sit around depressed and dejected. The daughters of Zelophehad could have sat in their tents and bemoaned their fate. Sitting around and fueling each other's "ain't it awful" attitude was a choice they had, but they didn't make it. Instead, with faith and courage, they stood up and God noticed!

Remember that standing up has its counterfeits. Stubbornness, arrogance, and pride can be mistaken for standing up. Being stubborn means that we refuse to listen to the truth while holding fast to our uninformed opinions. Standing up does require confidence, but it also mandates humility. These sisters did the right thing at the right time in the right way. They approached their leaders with confident humility. That's a tough standard to live up to in our society when so often the loudest and most aggressive voices seem to command the most attention. So, before you stand up, prepare yourself with the truth and humble yourself so that you will not have to experience the humiliation of ignorance and misplaced zeal.

These sisters stood up for what was right at the right time.

So can you. The choice is yours. Replace timidity with courage and distrust with faith. The old parent directive tape can play over and over in your mind, "Sit down and shut up." Or you can erase the tape and insert a new command, "Stand up and speak up." Speaking up is my next word for you. But right now, stand *up*! Timothy 5:7 (CEV) "For God has not given us a spirit of timidity . . ."

Stand *Up* Steps

- Replace timidity with courage.
- Substitute faith for distrust.
- Believe who God says you are, not what detractors label you.
- Find a stand up example for your life and receive their stand up DNA.
- Stand up with stand up people; stop sitting down with negative, "ain't it awful" folks.
- Leave the sitting chair of your past behind; decide your future, stand up, and walk.
- When you get "sick and tired of being sick and tired," don't give up . . . stand *up*!

CHAPTER 2

Speak Up!-------------------------

Your voice must be heard. Someone else speaking for you will never take the place of your speaking up for what's important. The truth is, there's *a time to be quiet and a time to speak up.*[1] You have to let your voice be heard. God has put something inside you that He wants others to know and to hear. Yes, there are times when silence is the best course of action. But silence isn't a lifestyle; it's a pause, a selah, as the Psalms describe, an opportunity to listen, reflect, contemplate, rest, and meditate—for letting things simmer. But, the time arrives when the stew is cooked and you have to share it with others. The key to having a voice and being heard is about not waiting for someone to discover you, but placing yourself where you can be discovered, where you can be heard.

Public speaking is one of the best skills that anyone can possess as they move up. Speaking up communicates many nonverbal messages like:

- "I am confident."
- "My thoughts are worth being heard."
- "I can clearly articulate my plan and direction."

- "I am the woman for the job."
- "Give my voice your attention. This is important!"
- "It's my time and my turn to be heard; I've been silent long enough."

The daughters of Zelophehad had their voices heard—not only by man but also by God. I was watching an episode of *The Apprentice,* hosted by Donald Trump. There were four remaining candidates and each had to make a verbal presentation. Their previous PowerPoint materials and accomplishments wouldn't win the day; what they said had to make an impact. Their presentations and what they articulated would determine whether they moved on to the next round or not. And some clearly failed because they couldn't adequately put their thoughts into words or present themselves well. Be prepared when you have your chance to speak up, just as Zelophehad's daughters did, so that your speaking up actually makes an impact and you move up!

Zelophehad's daughters were clearly pushing the envelope and working outside normal channels. In their day, women had no rights and few comforts. They worked tirelessly, endlessly without recognition or compensation to care for their mates and children—always serving others. Fathers planned their marriages for their daughters as a matter of economics, politics, or duty. Education wasn't available to them unless they were nobility or in wealthy families. They were regarded more as chattel than as human. In speaking up they were risking their father's possessions, their acceptance in their community, and their lives. I can only guess what gave them the boldness and courage to speak up. Here are a few of my musings about their plight that may also give you reason to speak up:

1. A just cause.
2. A family's future.
3. A good God.
4. It's just your time!

A just cause will ignite you. The daughters of Zelophehad had not been born to a rebellious or disloyal father. His name and lineage by all rights should be preserved. True, their father had been a nobody. But nobodies in particular deserve justice. God is known to do some of His best work on behalf of those who are voiceless, who have not been recognized or noticed by society. Only by speaking up can justice come to the weak, victimized, unnoticed, and unrecognized nobodies in life. This description of the Hebrews also fits the daughters of Zelophehad or the victims of injustice today:

Once you were less than nothing; now you are God's own. Once you knew very little of God's kindness; now your very lives have been changed by it.[2]

Knowing that God believes you to be somebody will ignite you to speak up when your cause is just and your motive is right.

A *family's future will unite you*. The sisters stuck together. Their future was in unity not division or independence. Their corporate unity gave them mutual support. They weren't alone. They discovered the power in the truth that "God sets the solitary into families."[3]

A *good God will incite you*. Knowing that God is good will incite you to act. All good gifts come from Him and His plans for you are good, not evil, to prosper you and give you a hope.[4] That means that you can move into the future with boldness and courage because God is at work for good in all things for those who love Him and who move and act according to godly purposes.[5] Before you move God has already made His move in your behalf. Focusing on the people and circumstances that are against you will only serve to silence you with fear or discourage, distract, or detour you from your divine destiny. Fixing your eyes on God's goodness will empower and incite you to speak up declaring that goodness for yourself and others just as Zelophehad's daughters did.

You may now feel something passionately and intensely. Speak up, girl! You may have an idea or vision that needs a voice. Speak up, son! Founder of the Roycroft Press, Elbert Green Hubbard, remarked, "To avoid criticism, do nothing, say nothing, be nothing." You may fear criticism, rejection, or ridicule for speaking up. Those who lack initiative, courage, and boldness often say nothing waiting for others to speak up so that they will have something to critique. Such cowardice doesn't deserve a moment of your attention or response. Step out and speak up. Never allow the possible mockery of others to stifle the importance of what you must say.

Fearlessly, Speak Up for Yourself!

Never let fear keep you from speaking up. You have nothing to fear. Your yeses are lining up. Your voice is tuning up. God hasn't given you a spirit of fear, but has imbued you with power, love, and a good, sound mind to give voice to your dreams, visions, ideas, and thoughts.[6] The fear of striking out may be keeping you out of the game. So what if you miss the mark with a speech or message? So what if you stumble a bit, mumble, or stutter? Find your voice. Failing to get the words out with great articulation the first time or first few times isn't failure. Keep at it. Prepare and get some training. Enroll in Toastmasters if you must. Tape yourself and listen to what you say over and over again to improve your communication. Even with twenty-five years of professional speaking under my belt, I still work at it. I often tape myself so I may be stronger not longer in my delivery. Obtain an online or CD course to build for yourself a Harvard vocabulary. Work on your diction. Work on your timing. Work on any lisp or speech deficiency you have. Work on your voice, presentation, substance, and style. Speak up.

Public speaking, speaking so that your voice can be heard in a confident way, is one of the best talents and gifts you can employ. But you have to hone that skill and then you have to use it. I had a wonderful moment while I was at Emerson College, my alma mater. I went first to be a speech therapist. I had been attracted to the school when I saw the front of the catalog where a young woman, probably a student, was helping a child wearing a hearing aid. She was teaching that child to speak, and that compassion drew me in. So I chose that school, and I started taking courses for speech and public speaking.

One of the courses was Oral Interpretation. I never knew what that was, but it was a required course taught by a woman named Frances LeShoto, who was the diva of oral interpretation on the East Coast. We had to do one scene where one person had to play all the characters in a scene. I chose one with three characters, a man, the mother of that man, and his teenage sister. It was the Lorraine Hansberry classic, *A Raisin in the Sun.* I had to play all three parts and use my voice to convince people that they were in the room with these different people.

When I was finished speaking, Mrs. LeShoto rose and gave me a standing ovation, and the greater portion of the class followed. I realized that I had a gift for oratory that I had not known I had. From that moment on, I asked God to let me make my living speaking. I wanted to use my voice to make my living, and that moment was a turning point for me. I have recently been contacted by the president of my alma mater and asked to serve on the board of directors to help this new generation of students. She said, "I've followed you closely for the past twenty-five years, and you have quite a reputation as a great speaker." What an honor.

Not long ago at a family gathering which was very public, my eleven-year-old son rose to speak for the first time. I had not heard him before, but it was clear that he had been working at it and absorbed some of my techniques when he went with me on the road. When he finished, the adult crowd of three hundred-plus stood just as my Oral Interpretation class had and it sent chills through me. He "wow-ed" them.

It's that simple. You can speak too. Start today. Encourage yourself and those around you to participate in family gatherings and to give tributes, blessings, and honor to one another. Start in your comfort zone, where you already have a support system. Then volunteer at your place of worship or at an event at work to speak up. Expand yourself. It's never too early or too late to start. Get a speech coach. But just start speaking. The Scriptures remind us that a person's gifts make room for him or her[7] and bring him or her before great men. At this writing, former president Bill Clinton accepted an invitation to a service I conduct in the Wall Street area. I was so excited that he would be coming to speak and then I got the message he wanted *me* to speak. I cannot tell you how important it is to practice speaking now. One never knows when someone will want you to speak for and to them. What an honor!

Everyone will have a turning point in their ability to speak up. Whether it's a presentation in a corporate boardroom, a talk before your family at a reunion, or a presentation in a classroom, there will come a time when you will have to present your thoughts clearly and concisely in a way that is so moving that others will be persuaded to think and act upon what you have said.

Speak Up for Others!

Zelophehad's daughters discovered that they had a voice for themselves and for future generations. Their speaking up not only secured an inheritance for themselves but also paved the way for their children and their children's children. Proverbs 31:8–9 reads, "Speak up for those who cannot speak for themselves for the rights of all that are destitute. Speak up and judge fairly. Defend the rights of the poor and needy." Being close to Coretta King and the Civil Rights movement, I have seen both women and men speak up to defend the rights of the disenfranchised and displaced, the poor and those persecuted.

God says that the poor are going to be among us always.[8] That's not just the poor financially. There will be those who don't have a voice and someone has to be a voice for the voiceless; those who have the resources, platform, and abilities to speak up. They must be that voice. I grew up in the midst of the Civil Rights movement. Born in 1957, I entered history at a time when there were "freedom schools," alternative free schools for African Americans. Ethnic minorities had great marches on Washington. Through the leaders of that time children learned what organizational and vocal skills were necessary for change and how to speak up for what was right. We benefited and the generations that followed also benefited. We must learn to speak up and also teach our children how to do so. Today we can witness a woman candidate for the presidency of the United States who has to speak publicly, sometimes without notice. I've also witnessed Marian Wright Edelman, founder of the Children's Defense Fund, speak up powerfully for impoverished children and make a lasting impact in our culture.

The Virtue of Boldly Speaking Up

As I mentioned in chapter 1, each *up* has an accompanying virtue integral to it. Arguably each up has a number of character traits that display themselves each time that up is demonstrated. Particularly noticeable with speaking up is the quality of boldness. This quality was noted by those observing the early church leaders as they proclaimed good news throughout the streets of Jerusalem without fear: "they spoke the word of God with boldness."[9]

Unashamed boldness. Boldness conveys much about the one who dares to speak up. Such a person isn't ashamed of whatever cause or message he or she advocates. One may quietly whisper words of gossip or deceit only into the ears of those inclined to conspire with them. But boldness dresses the speaker who confidently knows that her message is true and uncompromising. As I speak, teach, or preach my convictions, I am not ashamed of myself or the message that I proclaim. I may be in the halls of academia or among political adversaries who deride me and decry my words. But within me swells up a determination to speak up regardless of the personal price I may pay for the message. I must speak up with clear and undaunted and unashamed boldness.

Daring boldness. Speak up with *daring* boldness—the Apostle Paul calls this "all boldness."[10] As you dare to speak up, boldness rises within you providing fuel for the flames of your beliefs. To dare to speak up conveys a boldness that puts right above pleasing or placating those listening. As an immature speaker, I often wondered what people were thinking as I spoke. I would look for nonverbal signals from my audience conveying their favor, attentiveness, and agreement with me. My boldness would increase proportionate to their positive responses and decrease when they grew silent, frowned, or lost interest. Never allow the listeners to quench your boldness. Dare to be bold, seeking to please God rather than people.

Paul the Apostle certainly demonstrated this quality

as he often risked mob protests, arrests, and even death in preaching good news with daring boldness. His self-examining questions are ones we could ask ourselves. Paul wrote, "For do I now persuade men, or God? Or do I seek to please men? For if I still pleased men, I would not be a bondservant of Christ."[11] His passion for Christ filled him with a daring boldness that spoke up irrespective of any risk to his reputation or well-being.

The daughters of Zelophehad certainly exhibited a daring boldness as they spoke up in a male-dominated culture that could have put them away or stoned them without a second thought. Setting aside any thought of personal risk or danger, they spoke up to the male leader and shook the tradition inhibiting them and circumscribing their future. Daring boldness moved them into a posture of speaking up to claim their inheritance and their legacy. Who are you trying to please—a parent, spouse, child, boss, or friend? Pleasing them may keep you from boldly speaking up. Yet the very message that threatens them may become the words of truth that set both you and them free. The truth sets people free![12] So, with daring boldness, speak up with the truth.

Passionate boldness. We often find ourselves mired in insipid mediocrity. Popular speaker John L. Mason writes about "an enemy called average."[13] Banal lifestyles strip all passion from us. Our mindless routines of eating, sleeping, work, and pleasure-seeking entertainment become so normative that we fail to be passionately stirred by anything—good or evil. We choose preference over conviction and pastels over vivid colors. We disappear behind sameness fearing that if we are noticed, we might have to make passionate commitments that cost us both time and money while risking friendships and positions of power and influence. Where is the passionate street corner orator or preacher who dares to put herself up for ridicule and become the target of a tomato or two? Anglican clergyman John Wesley echoed such passion in his prayer, "Set me aflame so that people may watch me burn."[14] Speak up with passionate boldness!

At this writing, I have just returned from Washington, D.C., where CNN and a religious group, Sojourners, held the first faith forum for the top three Democratic presidential candidates. I was chosen to be one of only four questioners. Not only did I speak up, with confidence, I also wore bold, vivacious colors for TV, not drab clothing. For the one question I would ask, I practiced for two days. Millions watched. What a privilege.

Persistent boldness. With the first mocking look or laugh, will you sit down and shut up? Once you experience rejection or ridicule, will you shut up instead of speaking up? Persistence pushes through the flack of detractors and moves up instead of quitting or moving away from what needs to be said. Speaking up with boldness requires repeating your message over and over again and the freshness of its impact may become monotonous to you. So you must decide to press on even when you are tired of hearing yourself. Remember that your message is being heard for the first time by your new listeners even if you have spoken it hundreds of times. Even when the same people hear your same message over and over again, they can glean something new and revelatory if you persist. Persistence often leads to persuasion, which influences people to allow us to speak to new possibilities, with new invitations in new settings. So persistently speak up boldly!

Fearless boldness. You have nothing to fear, nothing to lose, and nothing to hide. What fear is it that keeps you silent? What fear is it that robs your voice of conviction and your audience of hearing truth? What fear is it that renders you dumb and inarticulate? Is it the fear of stumbling or stuttering? Of being rejected or ridiculed? The fear of being mocked or ignored? So what! Replace fear with boldness. Don't freeze up; free up. Let the flame of passion thaw you so that you will boldly speak up.

Creating a Legacy of Speaking Up

My first congregation was in what they call a working poor neighborhood on the Lower East Side of New York City. Many of the people who lived there were either third-generation public assistance families or were barely making it on their own. When one is in that survival mode, one does not always have time to dream or to speak. People were just trying to keep the little bit they had from being lost or stolen and to keep their families intact. That's why the roles of the minister and of the community leader are so important. It is important too that they walk in integrity and that they are able to verbalize on behalf of the ones who can't speak on their own behalf. In serving that community for thirteen years I saw people who had been empowered because I had spoken up to build up their self-esteem and skill while likewise equipping others to help people the same way.

We helped send people to college—the first to go in three generations or more—and they came back and began to help their own community. Many are still working on the Lower East Side right where they came from. After I had left the neighborhood, their new pastor came to visit me at my new congregation and shared about the leaders who had emerged over the years. This brought such joy to my heart. Many are now leaders in that church, on community boards, or employed in powerful positions. They are speaking up! What you do not only empowers you but the next generation. So we must be a voice.

Yes, I do come from a traditionally, historically deprived community, but we've learned to speak up because of the leadership of the Dr. Kings, the Adam Clayton Powells, the Coretta Scott Kings, and the Jesse Jacksons. Recently, talk-show host Don Imus said something racist about the Rutgers women's basketball team on air. People did speak up and the networks responded; Imus was fired. When people like that fuel hatred, we must speak up. When the poor have no resources or voice, we must speak up. When the downtrodden, uneducated, and powerless have no voice, we must speak up.

The leaders from my ethnic background found their voices and spoke up so that minorities from every background might claim their God-given rights and might also find their voices for justice. As you consider speaking up, ask yourself these questions:

- Why are you silent?
- Are you simply listening or is something else happening inside of you?

- Are you afraid?
- Afraid of being criticized or persecuted?
- Afraid of being rejected or ignored?
- Afraid for yourself or for your family's safety?
- What keeps you silent?

Your silence can be a travesty or become a tragedy; you or others may never move up if you fail to speak up. Review, remember, and rehearse all that you have learned in this chapter. Take the steps below and then, for God's sake and for the sake of others as well as yourself, speak *up*!

Speak *Up* Steps

- Pray and listen to God's leading and direction right now. Ask God to help you to "open your mouth and increase your territory" (prayer of Jabez in 1 Chronicles 4:10).

- Surround yourself with people who will affirm and support you. Go where you are celebrated, not tolerated. There are cheerleaders who have just been waiting for you to get into the game.

- Prepare what you are going to say and then practice articulating your message clearly. Start with your tape recorder, and practice in front of your mirror.

Listen to yourself. Look at yourself. Laugh at yourself. And then try again until you get the tone and attitude you are reaching for.

- Embrace a bold and courageous attitude. Your attitude determines your altitude. Be bold, honey. The New Testament says God gives us "holy boldness."

- Speak up and create an environment and legacy for others to speak up. Start working with those around you. It is very important to give young people a chance to start early. Last week a young woman in our church wrote a poem and we asked her to recite it before the congregation. She got an ovation. This was encouragement and practice all rolled into one. Many of the famous entertainers from our cultural traditions say they got their first public break in our houses of faith. I am in the process of creating the Moving Up Institute™—an endowment where others learn and train to speak up and move up—to do just that.

CHAPTER 3

Look Up! ----------------------------------

ou need a higher power. That's how I start it. That's how I finish it and everything in between. And that's what I stand on. Much talk exists about depending on a higher power, and how can one depend on a higher power as described in AA. When you look up to a higher power, you are reaching out to God. I believe God wants you to know that He is very much present to you and accessible by you. In fact, his promise is this: "Seek me and live."[1]

The great thing about living in the now is that you don't have to go through anyone else to get to God— your higher power, connection, and source. Just plug into Him. Not only do you not have to go through anyone, you do not have to wait on anyone or get permission from anyone. Start now. God's been waiting to make your acquaintance.

In today's convenience-driven culture, we have many time-saving appliances like toasters, washers, micro-waves, and vacuum cleaners, but unless they're plugged in, they're useless and simply taking up space. When we plug them in, connecting them to a power source, then we're able to have wonderful baked breads, clean homes, and other amenities that will help in and enhance our daily lives.

Well, that's what has to happen to us—body, soul, and spirit. We must look up to hook up and connect with our higher power, who gives us our ability and strength to continue on through every situation in life. The shepherd king David sang about the secret of looking up:

> *I will look up to the mountains—*
> *does my help come from there?*
> *My help comes from the LORD,*
> *who made the heavens and the earth!*[2]

Having the spiritual connection with God means you are looking up to God for your sustenance, strength, and help in everything. The daughters of Zelophehad were very clear that they needed to be connected to a higher power. It says very clearly in the text that they went and they stood by the door of the tabernacle of meeting, the place where Moses met with God face to face.[3] We would equate that place today with the church sanctuary. That's where the power is. Don't be so busy doing PowerPoint that you forget the point of power.

Those sisters would have looked up and seen the cloud of God's presence, a cloud by day and fire by night, suspended over the tent of meeting. They put themselves in a position to look up and see the source of their strength and power. They desired to connect with more than just a man, Moses. They wanted an encounter with God. So they looked up.

Look Up and Connect with God

It's one thing to learn PowerPoint but you also need to be connected to a point of power and that power is God. We spend a lot of time on technological advancement. What I'm trying to do is motivate people to also have theological and spiritual advancement in their lives to couple with, complement, and accompany that technical power. I think this is why we see the demise of so many of the stars who have accumulated so much materially. They acquired it very quickly and at such a young age; they have an abundance of stuff but lack an abundance of life. You can't connect with stuff; you must be connected to the source and Creator in order to have meaning in life.

I wish I could have had a conversation, and maybe I still can, with a Britney Spears, Paris Hilton, Lindsay Lohan, or a Nicole Richie, who, by media accounts, all seem to be falling apart at the seams. They have everything materially that we could imagine. They have millions and billions of dollars but they're still asking, "How do I stay connected?" They seem to be disconnected from the power source. My advice to them would be that you need a connection to God. That's what keeps you grounded when you're on the road and when there's all the lights and the action and the cameras and you're not sure who's around you. One certainty we have is that God is unchangeable and that He is present whether we are in a Hollywood limo or on the local bus going to work. I love the way the psalmist describes His presence:

O LORD, you have examined my heart
and know everything about me.
You know when I sit down or stand up.
You know my every thought when far away.
You chart the path ahead of me
and tell me where to stop and rest.
Every moment you know where I am.
You know what I am going to say
even before I say it, LORD.
You both precede and follow me.
You place your hand of blessing on my head.
Such knowledge is too wonderful for me,
too great for me to know!

I can never escape from your spirit!
I can never get away from your presence!
If I go up to heaven, you are there;
if I go down to the place of the dead, you are there.
If I ride the wings of the morning,
if I dwell by the farthest oceans,
even there your hand will guide me,
and your strength will support me.[4]

What we have to learn is how to have this flow within our lives. One of my male friends says that at a certain point life is like a dance, and we learn to flow with God, with one another, and with ourselves. There is a tri-une God—Father, Son, and Holy Spirit—and we are tri-une in that we are mind, body, and spirit. We have been created in three parts. However, in life we are generally taught how to focus on mainly one part, particularly accentuating the mind. We have been taught to firm up the body. The commercials scream at you to eat right, stay fit, and to buy the products that will shape up, support, and firm up your body. But there is also spiritual health and there is only one way that you can get spiritually connected and that is through the spiritual source which is the Spirit of God. I call it my "watching the waves dance" moment.

Take Time to Look Up

To look up means taking the time to find a place within yourself and around you to renew your spirit. Be intentional. That's what *insight* means—you have taken the time to look within. Set a time with a friend or a coworker or a peer to be with God. Take a spiritual health break. You might pray, speak a Scripture passage to one another or even read a devotional book to one another. Let me share with you an example of what I mean.

We went on a tour to South Africa a few years ago. Thirteen days into the trip I was saturated with looking at tourist sights. Instead of taking another bus tour on the next day, I decided to stay at the hotel. Being close to the coast, I simply walked by the shore and found a place to look up. I just sat there and watched the waves that day. I saw the different formations of the waves, the foam spray, and the tide coming in and going out. As I sat watching the waves, at that particular moment, God and I had a major encounter.

Water is one of the things that soothes my spirit and soul. God and I met at that moment and I was connected to my spiritual source. For as certainly as God made the water and the waves, "The earth is the Lord's and the fullness thereof . . . for he hath founded it upon the seas."[5]

And as certainly as He can speak to the winds and the waves, God can and will also speak to us when we seek him. Let me invite you:

Look up from the busyness and treadmill of work and tasks . . .

Look up from the disturbing pettiness of detractors and distractions . . .

Look up from the mundane and routine . . .

Look up from the sitcoms and talk shows that clutter the airways with meaningless chatter . . .

Look up from the empty calories of daily life and feast at a table set before you . . .

Look up and feed on the bread of life that gives sustenance far beyond health foods.

Looking up is about being intentional in eating soul food. Such soul food is filled with nutrients and supplements that will enhance all parts of your life. I watch a lot of *Entertainment Tonight* and *Access Hollywood* because my first career was TV. So I like to watch those Hollywood dramas a lot and what I'm beginning to see is the stars are starting to say things like, "When I'm on the road, you know I have my manager and I have my businessperson and I have my PR person but I also need my spiritual leader." So you see Madonna's fascination with a kabbalist rabbi and rap stars including ministers in their entourages. Denzel Washington and others openly go to church with their families. What people are realizing is the only thing that keeps us grounded is that spiritual connection found in looking up. So I urge people to look up, look up to the Lord and find strength beyond human effort.

Looking Up Inspires Hope

Never underestimate the power of hope. Looking down brings you to a point of depression. Looking down keeps you from looking ahead. Hope sees beyond the present situation into the possibilities of what's next. Without a next, hope disperses into nothingness.

At times throughout my life, I have wanted to give up instead of looking up. I have been tempted to let go of my dreams and abort my visions. Discouraged by circumstances and disappointed by people, I felt hopeless, helpless, and alone. Yet, I wasn't alone. God whispered to me in a still, small voice, "I will never leave you or forsake you."[6]

Reinhold Niebuhr once made a remark saying faith is a citadel of hope built on the brink of despair. Looking up starts with trusting God and results in birthing hope. Hope is a confident expectation that even when I have reached the end of my rope, I can look up and see a rescue rope within my grasp extended by the One above and beyond me. God is my hope.[7]

Hope expects the unexpected, believes the unbelievable, and imagines the unimaginable. How is that possible? Within myself, my own strength, knowledge, and understanding, I have a finite view of my problems and my solutions. I need to look up in order to look beyond the immediate moment into the future possibilities. Without future possibilities, I have nowhere to turn and no place to go. I am stuck in the rut of my past so much that my past determines my future. But by looking up, I put my hope in someone other than myself or those around me, who so easily fail to keep their promises.

Consider again the daughters of Zelophehad. Daddy had died and with him the material hope of an inheritance. So what were they to do? Sit around in their tents and weep? Badmouth the traditions set by men? Have a "male-bashing" session? Refuse to make any future plans? Have a pity party? No way. By looking up they seized hope for an inheritance. God honored their speaking up when they had the inner fortitude to look up.

I had a friend who deeply disappointed me. I counted on her to be there for me when I needed her. Instead, she turned against me at the worst possible time in my ministry. If I had chosen to focus on her failures or my own disappointments, I would have lost all hope and may even have left my ministry. But disappointment always looks back instead of looking up. Looking up moves us up beyond where we are to a new place of possibility and hope.

Hope means I can expect God to do what I can't, lead in ways I don't understand, and reveal new things I've never imagined. Looking down births depression; looking up inspires hope. Lift up your eyes to the hills. Look away from the one who has hurt you. Look up into the face of the One who loves you. When all is dark around you and no light shines at the end of your tunnel of despair, look up! St. Paul writes about looking up into His face this way:

> For God, who said, "Let there be light in the darkness," has made us understand that this light is the brightness of the glory of God that is seen in the face of Jesus Christ.
>
> But this precious treasure—this light and power that now shine within us—is held in perishable containers, that is, in our weak bodies. So everyone can see that our glorious power is from God and is not our own.
>
> We are pressed on every side by troubles, but we are not crushed and broken. We are perplexed, but we don't give up and quit. We are hunted down, but God never abandons us. We get knocked down, but we get up again and keep going.[8]

Knocked down? Look up. Perplexed and confused? Look up. Surrounded by trouble, in despair and depressed? Look *up*!

Don't Dilute Your Search for God

I want to add one other thing about looking up. I often speak to corporate groups. Initially, I thought I had to taint my message to speak to corporate America. I would finish my conversations having talked only of business and stop short of making any reference to looking up. Then I'd receive a follow-up communication that sounded something like this: "We know you can talk about being a businessperson but what we would really like is for you to do some spiritual coaching with our leaders because that's what their souls need and that's what they're asking for. They can't always ask openly but that's what they need so, if you wouldn't mind, we really need you to be a pastor in our presence." So the soul is constantly seeking its source; the soul is constantly seeking its God. What we have to do is make a place for the soul and God to meet.

How do we do that? It's not an easy pursuit, but it is so rewarding when one takes the time and makes the effort to look up. Instead of telling you just one way that works for me, I want to give you a list of twenty-one ways to look up. These are simple, practical ways to look up. Not all of them are for everyone. But one or two or more will work for you in making a place for your soul and God to meet.

Ways to Look Up

1. **Pray**. Set aside a quiet time to pray regularly. Talk with God as you would a friend. Start each day praying, "Good morning, dear God, I am here and ready to report for duty. What would you have me to do today?" Start with an affirmation such as, "This is the day the Lord has made, let us rejoice and be glad in it."

2. **Study**. The Scriptures admonish us "to study to show thyself approved."[9] There are exciting Bible studies taking place sometimes in your office or at lunchtime in other venues. Be in a guided class at first until you are sure you know how to navigate the Scriptures yourself.

3. **Share**. The best way is the group way. Whenever I share in a group, I also find myself receiving something in return. We close our worship services each week in our church with the words in a chorus, "I Need You to Survive."[10] This powerful song speaks of the needs we all have for sharing and fellowship.

4. **Contemplate**. Take time to listen and reflect. One of

my favorite books is *The Genessee Diary* by Henri Nouwen. He shares how he was led by the spirit into a contemplative life and in his seventh year of a busy pastorate checked himself into a Jesuit monastery. Most of us don't have to go to that extreme, but there are days when I check myself into a retreat center or hotel room. I pull away from the busyness of life and bask in God's presence. Nouwen wrote about becoming so busy lecturing about prayer that he had stopped praying. Could that be where you find yourself at this moment? Too busy to pray? Stop. Pray. Contemplate and meditate.

5. **Meditate**. When Joshua was beginning his new leadership role and was moved up to leader, Scripture reports that he was commanded to meditate on the word of God.[11] He chewed mentally and spiritually on God's law. He digested the meat of God's word for his life. What is your meditation for this day?

6. **Read**. To move up you must not only look up but also book up. As the public service announcement declares, *a mind is a terrible thing to waste*. Pull away from your TV or iPod. Decide that you will read a book that will inspire and equip you to look up.

7. **Study**. Life is a journey of learning with burning and yearning. We are students for life. Seek out a group through your community college, local house of worship, or regional adult education center for studying religion,

philosophy, language, and the arts. Let everything from books, music, theater, and the study of the arts expand your capacity to look up.

8. **Sing**. Each of us, as world-renowned leader Jim Forbes says, has a song inside of us. Go ahead and sing your song. Let your song out that's been inside of you. Sing your favorite song today.

9. **Walk**. Walk by faith and not by sight. Get up and walk; don't just sit around bemoaning your problems. You may be committed in your fitness routine to walking. Use that walking time for thinking, meditating, praying, and communing with God. Look up as you walk.

10. **Be still and silent**. God commands, "Be still and know that I am God."[12] Out of stillness comes the voice of God's will to our spirits. I have visited homes and noticed that the residents never turned off a TV, radio, or CD player. They had to surround themselves with noise 24/7. Rarely did they take time to be still and silent. Consequently, their attention was always on what others chose for them to see or hear instead of what God was speaking to them. Take a vacation from electronic intrusions. Look up.

11. **Create**. If you don't see it, create it. Our ancestors did not have what we have; they had to create it. Being created in God's image, we have a divine imprint on our lives to be like Him. He creates; we create.

12. **Dream**. Don't dismiss your dreams. They come from God. A dream is the roadway to your destiny. Recently I saw this quote: "Dreams do not have an expiration date."

13. **Vision**. *Vision* is the root word of "visionary." All those who will move up must be able to see where they are going. All great leaders are visionaries. They see the extraordinary, not the ordinary. Ask God for a vision for your life.

14. **Declare**. Declare today that this is the first day of the rest of your life and that the best is yet to come. Declare, "It is my time and turn. I have been prepared for this moment. I will seize it and squeeze it. Today is different than yesterday. I will not go back, look back, nor turn back. I'm moving up!"

15. **Confess**. Come to God. Ask for forgiveness and then don't pick that offense up again.

16. **Repent**. Say, "God, I am sorry. Put me on the road toward you. Take me out of darkness into the marvelous, new light. I'm tired of messing up. I'm ready to move up."

17. **Change**. **It begins now**! Change is rarely comfortable or expected. In fact, change expects the unexpected. It's like sandpaper smoothing out the rough edges of your personality or irritation creating pearls in your attitudes.

18. **Renew**. Choose to become new again. The old is passing away and the new is coming.[13] Be prepared for

the new. Embrace the new. Allow God to do a "new thing" in you (Isaiah 43).

19. **Revive**. "Because the resurrected Christ lives, I live and can face my tomorrows with faith and without fear." Say this over and over again.

20. **Give**. You have freely received; so give freely.

21. **Listen**. God has been speaking to you all along your path. Now hear and obey what he has to tell you. Remember that the daughters of Zelophehad were ready to look up when they were stirred up to move up.

22. **Watch the Waves Dance**. Find your place and time to do absolutely nothing. Elizabeth Gilbert calls it *"la vida dulce nuovo"*—the sweet new life.

In looking up, don't be frustrated. You can't make yourself religious and God isn't interested in your religious ritual. Your desire is God's—a relationship that lifts you up above weakness into strength; above the ordinary into the extraordinary; above the natural into the supernatural; above the drudgery into the delight of God's joy. Take a step of faith . . . look *up*!

CHAPTER 4

Book Up!------------------------------

S ome of my most memorable moments with my mother and grandmother were the nighttime bedtime stories. With great joy and fascination, books took me to places I had never been. Not only was my comprehension expanded, but also my knowledge, imagination, and inspiration. I am still a reader today and the impact is still great. In a world of technology, please don't lose the art of reading a good book. (You've got a great one in your hands right now.)

Reading is leading. No leader can lead without having read and learned from books, both classic and contemporary. Books empower leaders with knowledge in moving up toward a leadership position. They are moving up from where they are to a new level of growth. Wherever my journey has taken me, it has been important to find out what those in the know were thinking and reading. When I left for my first White House position as a domestic policy analyst, one of my dear friends asked me, "What's the culture of the White House? What are they reading now? I believe it is the *Culture of Disbelief* by Stephen Carter." Sure enough, when I got to the White House, that was the book. After reading it, I was able to enter into dialogue on many occasions because I had expanded my library to include a book that was meaningful to and for that context. Moving up requires booking up. Read up—this chapter is just for you.

Expand your reading list to expand your thoughts and mind-set. David Wilkerson, in *The Prayer of Jabez,* quotes this spiritual prayer:

> Oh, that You would bless me indeed, and enlarge my territory, that Your hand would be with me, and that You would keep me from evil, that I may not cause pain![1]

Books enlarge your territory and take you places you could never physically visit. They expand your knowledge, creativity, and imagination. The knowledge you gain can lead you to liberation and strength.

What to Read

You need to begin to read the periodicals and the publications of the industry you're trying to pursue. Read the biographies of great winners. I said earlier that I always read the biographies of people like the hotel magnates, Marriott or Hilton. I enjoyed seeing how they built their dreams. I read the biographies of people who had visions and implemented them. I read the stories of great achievers and how they were raised to be champions, like Tiger Woods. I also read the stories about places I want to visit and experience, places that inspire even though I may never actually go there. Books empower us to vicariously experience what others have learned so that we don't have to reinvent the wheel every time we set out on a new life adventure.

Reading allows us to continue achieving and growing. I want to know about life. Success is not just about triumph. I want to know what trials people faced and how they overcame them. How did they rebound when they were knocked down? There are days when we're not feeling up, we're speaking up, we're looking up, we're booking up, but we're not feeling up. Well, how do we get through these times of transition and go from a trial to a triumph? How do we go from being a victim to a victor? How do we go from being miserable to fulfilling a mission in life? We can find the answers in books.

In reading the story of Zelophehad's daughters in Numbers 27, I was booking up. They inspired me and gave birth to this book. Their story lifted me up to consider greater and higher possibilities and potential for my life . . . and for yours! Here are some interesting facts about the Bible.

On Wikipedia, the online encyclopedia, a list of the world's bestselling books is published.[2] The first book ever printed was the Gutenberg Bible; before that texts were hand copied through the centuries by scribes, monks, and scholars. It is estimated that 6.7 billion have been printed. Begin booking up by reading Scripture. The American Bible Society as well as the United Bible Societies around the world have wonderful reading programs that can take you through the Bible in a year.

Literacy is one of my priority issues. People have their electronic toys that entertain them. They substitute pleasure for learning and replace knowledge with pop trivia. I know because my sons and my husband have filled my house with gadgets to view videos, listen to music, and play games. They'll come in the door and pick up a gadget and play a game.

I want to see you play a book, I want to see what you can tell me about what you're thinking and comprehending about this book. Even then schools assign summer reading, and I enjoy seeing their minds expand with literature they would not have chosen on their own. Books can take you to a new level. Tell me what's in a person's library and I can tell a lot about that person. Oprah has been encouraging people to read for years. She is on the right path.

I encourage people to read to increase their knowledge and to increase the places they can go. Years ago, I had a philosophy professor, Dr. Cornel West, who is now at Princeton. In my first class with him he said, "My books go where I can't physically get. So people in Africa and North Korea can read my stories even if they've never met me in person and in doing that I'm helping someone to aim a little higher." I will never forget that. Reading is so important; it really is fundamental and it is fun.

The Legacy of Reading

My mother was a schoolteacher and she taught at a wonderful school, the Countee Cullen School, P.S. 194, in Manhattan, a wonderful community school in the village of Harlem, named after one of the Harlem Renaissance's great poets. There were a number of black and Jewish teachers who had close relationships. They started collecting books for us. Every new book that came out was in our library and new encyclopedias came out that accented and affirmed our heritage. My mother brought them home. It was fascinating to read about and see photos of historical places and figures who informed and shaped my thinking. It was intense and so as a third grader I was reading books like *Letters from a Birmingham Jail.*

I read Martin Luther King's book *Where Do We Go from Here: Chaos or Community?* It fascinated me. Then when I was in fourth grade my mother took me to Hunter College because Dr. Martin Luther King was going to speak there. Having read some of his works I connected with the man, and I think that's when my destiny really began. When he finished speaking, he came to the edge of the stage and I told him I was reading his book and he said, "Really?" I said, "Yes." I had my book with me and he signed an autograph for me. But meeting a world-class leader and having read as much of his book as I could comprehend was what propelled me as an adult to read all of his writings. I won't forget that moment, and because of my parents and the library they created, I read up.

Before she died, Coretta Scott King, Dr. King's widow, invited me to preach the last King service at Ebenezer Baptist Church, the church where Dr. King had preached. It happened to be the last King memorial service that she was present at in January 2005, on the national holiday weekend in which we celebrate Dr. King's birthday. She insisted on giving me many autographed books from her personal library. At the time I was thinking to myself, This is a heavy load of books to carry. But she must have known intuitively that she would not be alive much longer and she wanted me to have a piece of her priceless library and a piece of her. How grateful I am that I now have collector items in my library. It's so meaningful to sit and read them and have them for my children—books are a legacy.

My first church was Mariners Temple, the oldest Baptist Church in New York City, on the Lower East Side of New York City. I had a library of wonderful books, many of them personally signed, like one by Harry Emerson Fosdick who was one of the great preachers of the twentieth century. It's fascinating to read the insights of all those people, and I was in the midst of greatness in all these books.

I also read the *Crain's Business* report, because I am in New York and have a church service on Wall Street on Wednesdays at lunchtime. So, if I am to work in the Wall Street community, I need to know what businesspeople are reading, thinking, and talking about. So I read *Crain's,* I read the *Wall Street Journal,* and I read various financial publications from around the world. The *Wall Street Journal* has become one of my favorite papers. At first glance it can appear to be very dry and heavy material, but I find the writing credible and the headlines are always great. It allows me to relate to the community that I serve. I can't always spend my lunch hour or happy hour with my congregants but I can connect with them through these papers.

Curiosity Inspires Booking Up

Books, like salt, make you thirsty for more—more knowledge, understanding, and insight. Becoming a learner for life actually takes effort on our parts. Think of the books you've bought but never read or started but never finished.

Some say that most books bought are never read all the way through. I know that's right! With all good intentions, I buy these interesting books in airport stores or at conferences, but I never get around to reading all of them. Oh, I start most of them and even get a few chapters into them, but then pressures, distractions, and interruptions press in. So I dog-ear the page fully expecting to pick up where I stopped but never getting around to it. Woe is me.

Yet, months later, I may see that book just lying there on the side table beckoning to me. Curiosity prompts me to open it up. The companions of curiosity are imagination and fascination. I want to know more. My imagination gets stirred by the possibilities pictured in a book. I travel around the world without leaving my chair or when I go to a place I've read about the history helps it to come alive! I see things in my mind that no picture or photo can ever capture. I wonder about things that I had never even thought about before. Curiosity makes an explorer out of me. The same will happen for you. I'm finding now that because of my busy travel schedule that airplanes are a great place to read amid the clouds as I create a quiet space for myself.

I understand that the daughters of Zelophehad didn't have books to read. But they were curious. They imagined a culture and tradition different than the one they had inherited. They were curious about what life could be like with an inheritance that they might possess. The future they perceived for themselves as women was different than the one perceived for them by the men and perhaps other women around them. With the virtue of curiosity inspired by imagination and perhaps fueled by fascination, they questioned what was and saw other possibilities. They could see a future different for their daughters than the one they had inherited. Curiosity took them to a higher lifestyle.

Just reading about them has inspired me and I hope it has done the same for you. Reading the Book prompts me to see the invisible, hear the incredible, and attempt to do the impossible. Filled with God-given curiosity and imagination, I move to other books that reveal to me the biographies of people, the wonders of science, the marvels of travel, and the intricacies of business as well as the fiction of imagination. All of that opens up for me from reading. The same will happen for you when you book up!

Start Now!

How do you book up? You start reading—anything, anytime, anywhere. Not just thrilling novels but also nonfiction books and biographies that can inspire and inform you. At the end of this chapter, I will give you some book up steps that will help you get started or go deeper. You will never move up until you book up.

I suggest you read some of the following books right now. First, I recommend my first book with Doubleday, *Live Like You're Blessed.* Then read *The Success Principles* by Jack Canfield; it inspired me to book up even more. Next, read and ingest *The Wounded Healer* by Henri Nouwen, a Jesuit priest. Also read Nouwen's *The Genessee Diary.* I read this book when I was on sabbatical. It was a time in life when I was running down instead of moving up. Nouwen wrote about how he, as a leader in the church, was doing more talking about praying than actual praying, and he listed all the things that had taken him away from his first love, which was ministry. For a person on a sabbatical, burned out, needing a selah, a rest, a pause, it's a great book to read. It allows you to slow down; you can even put it down, think on it, and then pick it up again when you need it.

It's time for you to book up. Don't just buy a book and put it on the shelf. Take it with you. Read whenever you have a break, or when you are riding on a subway, bus, or as a passenger in a car or on a plane. I read and receive some of my best up inspiration on planes. Grab a few moments each day to read. Go on a trip without ever leaving home. Discover a new world of imagination, reality, and mindsets. Expand your territory: book *up*!

Book *Up* Steps

- Choose a book of nonfiction or biography to read right now and start reading.
- Set a time each day to read, even if it's just for five or ten minutes.
- Decide on a business or professional journal or paper to read weekly or even daily.
- Read classical authors as well as contemporary ones.

- Talk with a pastor, teacher, or professional about books they are reading. Find out their favorites and then read.

- Set a reading goal to book up for yourself. Perhaps reading one journal a week and one book a month will be a good start, and then increase that.

- Read Scripture regularly. You might start with a psalm or a chapter of Proverbs each day. Try a time for reading through John's Gospel or James's letter. Get a translation of the Bible that is easy for you to read like the New International Version, The New Living Translation, or my favorite, The Contemporary English Version.

Start your list of books to read today and keep track of your progress. Collect suggestions from others on your path and see what has helped them to be propelled to where they are now.

CHAPTER 5

Kiss Up! ----------------------------------

ave a negative reaction when I say, "Kiss *up*"? It doesn't have to be negative. Let me explain. "Kiss up" means that I understand who and what I'm up against, and I also understand that I need to move within this structure. I must learn who the players are, find favor with them, and find a friend among them. It's just wisdom. Zelophehad's daughters understood this well. They went first to Moses, and then there was a clear strategy of who to go to next.

When I first started going to Hampton University ministers' conferences, where I would later become their first female president, twenty-six years ago, there were only about ten female pastors in the country who had any kind of visibility or notoriety, and I was one of them. So when we went on campus it created a buzz among the men. Yes, men can and do talk. Women might call it gossip; men call it "talking in the parking lot," or like they did at Hampton, "talking under the big tree." The big tree was the famous meeting place for discussion on campus. Back then women church leaders were an anomaly, or a novelty.

In 1983 over five thousand preachers came together for the conference but only a few hundred were women. This less than four percent minority was looked at, talked about, undervalued, and usually were kept far away from positions of influence or pulpits of prestige. So we, the women pastors, would make the circuit, listen well, connect, and relate while spying out what we were up against.

There were many celebrity preachers and after each of the main sessions, young preachers would gather at the side and backstage entrances, just to get a glimpse, and perhaps a handshake if you were very fortunate. I joined the crowd. So much excitement abounded, especially after a great session. People's energies and emotions would be up.

I can remember putting my hand out to greet a man of position and power to introduce myself. Yes, I was kissing up because I had seen everybody flock to this person and I knew this person was a person of influence. I wanted to meet and get to know him and for him to know *me*. I knew this person had seen me enough times and I felt like he was ready to know who I was. When I held out my hand to introduce myself, rejection filled the atmosphere as he pushed my hand away and said, "I know who you are."

Now I didn't get an attitude like, "I'm never coming

back" or "I'm not going to speak to this person ever again." Instead, over a period of time, in fact twenty-three years of attending the conference, I continued to kiss up. I might have a meal with many of the male preachers or pass the well-known preacher who pushed my hand aside in the hallway and greet him as he stood among them. At times our hotels were the same and we would be on the same floor. And I would always speak. I began to know his family and would greet them and others. I began to find out some of the men at the conference played tennis and basketball and joined them, since I loved sports. Seeing me interact with various colleagues and peers through sports and other activities, this leader who had initially rejected me began to notice that I wasn't pushy or disrespectful; I was connecting in a positive, intentional way. I would hug those that I thought were genuinely open and receiving of hugs. That hug was a positive way to shake hands in my own personal way. Many of the older men began referring to me as their daughter, so daughter I would be. Now it was genuine kissing up because relationships were beginning to develop, and a hug or kiss is a way of expressing our care and admiration and positive affirmation of others. Especially in the African American and Italian cultures, to not kiss or hug means there's a distant relationship or none at all.

I kissed up for twenty-three years. Then, in the twenty-fourth year, the very person who had rejected my hand years before became instrumental in my election and elevation and was one of the people who walked me into a solemn assembly as the first female president of Hampton University. No more standing at the side or back entrances. I would walk and ride in the front. He was the one who orchestrated the politics behind the scenes and said, "You don't even need to know what goes on in the back room. We'll take care of it because you'll be operating as the first lady president."

Kissing up is simply connecting intentionally and positively. It is not a sign of weakness but relatedness. It is reaching out to others who might never reach out to you. It is being willing to meet the needs of others without compromising who you are. It's really loving God and others while still loving yourself. That's called the two great commandments. I call it *great commandment living through kissing up.*

Live a Kind Life

The character virtue integral to kissing up is kindness. Scripture actually commands, "Be kind to one another."[1] Some people have said to me, "Oh, you're really kissing up. You want something, so you're kissing up." Well, I think we should be sweeter and kinder in more areas, maybe in all areas, of our lives. You know today we seem to have to develop "an edge" to survive. But that edge isn't aggression; it's kindness.

Kissing up gives you an edge—a home-court advantage, as they say in sports—in building relationships that will bless you and others in the long term. How is that? In kissing up, you take the initiative and set the ground rules for building the relationship. You decide when and where and how you will connect. You see kissing up as connecting with kindness—a divine appointment instead of an opportunity to manipulate or dominate. Yes, you have an agenda, but it's good, not evil, just like God's agenda for us:

> "For I know the plans I have for you," declares the LORD, "plans to prosper you and not to harm you, plans to give you hope and a future. Then you will call upon me and come and pray to me, and I will listen to you. You will seek me and find me when you seek me with all your heart."[2]

When we have a good plan to connect with another person with a constructive agenda in mind, we don't have to be aggressive, crude, or rude. We can use the cutting edge of kindness. Kissing up is being aware of your edge and aware of why you are connecting. We need to be in *alignment* with God's plans and purposes. He knows the people who are to be in your life to help equip and empower you in your journey. I am convinced that we are to come into agreement with God's plans and purposes and agree with those with whom God connects us so that "His will in heaven can be done on earth." The Bible says, "Do unto others as you would have others do unto you."³ That is the Golden Rule and it's correct. In fact we really need to go for it.

What Does Kissing Up Kindness Really Look Like?

Kindness isn't spineless submission or superficial flattery. Kindness when expressed with sincerity really comforts and supports others and helps you to feel good as well. Kindness has no expectation of return or reward. It's unmerited favor or graciousness extended to others not because of who they are but because of who you are. A common cliché is *Mercy is getting what you don't deserve while grace is getting what you can never earn.* In a real sense, kindness combines both mercy and grace to the measure that humans are able to look beyond the faults and weaknesses of one another while willingly and cheerfully kissing up.

Kissing up is being kind even when the other person slams or persecutes us for no good reason. It's blessing those who really seek to do us wrong or do us in. It's living like you're blessed, as I wrote in my first book. In other words, you can choose to be kind and bless others regardless of how they treat you. Blessings are in store for those who choose to be kind, to kiss up, regardless of the attitude or actions of others. Jesus spoke of such blessings this way:

> God blesses those who realize their need for him,
> for the Kingdom of Heaven is given to them.
> God blesses those who mourn,
> for they will be comforted.
> God blesses those who are gentle and lowly,
> for the whole earth will belong to them.
> God blesses those who are hungry and thirsty for justice,
> for they will receive it in full.
> God blesses those who are merciful,
> for they will be shown mercy.
> God blesses those whose hearts are pure,
> for they will see God.
> God blesses those who work for peace,
> for they will be called the children of God.
> God blesses those who are persecuted because they live for God,
> for the Kingdom of Heaven is theirs.[4]

We receive what we see. If we want kindness and mercy, we proactively give it. Kissing up sows seed for a harvest. Not every seed sown brings a return.[5] Some seed never sprouts. Other seed springs up only to wilt and die. Some grows at first but is later choked out by weeds. But some seed takes root and bears fruit. Scripture refers to it as "falling on good ground." Not everyone we kiss up to will someday respond. That's not the issue. Kindness flows out of who we are not how others respond! So, kiss up! A blessing will always come not from the recipient of kindness but from the source—God.

Resolve to Be Kind

A few years ago, I woke up and said to myself, I'm going to make a resolution. Most everyone makes New Year's resolutions and finds them hard to keep. I wanted to make a resolution I could keep and this was it: *I'm going to be nice. I'm going to work at it. I will be intentional about it. If I find myself slipping, I'm going to apologize and I'm going to go back and do things correctly.*

For me, being nice or kind required an attitude transformation. The Bible says, "Be not conformed to this world but be transformed by the renewing of your mind."[6] In order to be kind and nice to people, I had to unlearn the negative, survival instincts of a New Yorker. We live in a city of around nine million people who fight for their space and pay dearly for it. But I don't need to fight with the world, I don't need to bust up others; I need to kiss up. So I made it my business to start kissing up. To take time to hear people, to look them in the eye, so when they said something like, My mother died, I didn't just say, Oh, that's too bad, and just keep moving. Instead I would stop and take the time to listen. President Bill Clinton has this gift. He makes each person he talks to feel like their issue and concern is important. I have seen him in a room of thousands, but he makes whoever he's engaged with feel special.

That's kissing up. It means to be intentional about being nice and about having charisma and a countenance that draws people and does not turn people off. It's about your facial expressions and nonverbal communication as well. I had someone in my office who had signed up to be the spearhead for a certain event. I saw her facial expression in the office one day and I said, "You don't look like you want to do this." And she said, "Oh, everybody tells me that. I really do want to do it." "But your body and your face don't say that."

So we began to work with her. It was done in love, not by putting her down, and she began to be cognizant of how her body language and facial expressions were being read. What I would do to begin to break down her edge was I would give her a hug when I saw her at the office. She had other issues in her life and I knew she just needed a little embrace. She has softened up and has become this little wonderful queen whom I and others enjoy being around, and we discovered some gifts we never knew she had. There has been a visible change in her countenance.

The Daughters of Zelophehad Kissed Up

In every culture, there is protocol and structures and that's why I wrote the Sister's Rules for Ministry.[7] Coming into the ministry as a female—and we're still a novelty to some of the men—I learned that one must know the rules and that often it's better to get men to let us in instead of pushing our way into the game.

You must learn the rules of the game; you have to learn the structures and how to navigate through them sweetly so people will want to invite you into a relationship. You must learn this if you are to accelerate and excel and if you are to not only get in, but stay in and survive.

The women in our story, the daughters of Zelophehad, understood very clearly the principles of protocol. The emerging Hebrew culture had the Law.

Men and women had their places. Authority and leadership had to be respected. They went to Moses first, and they went to the priests because you had to have a spiritual connection; they went to the tribal leaders, which showed they understood how to submit to authority, and they went to the congregation because there's also an accountability factor. Each of those steps had a different role in the process. They had to get the blessing of each of those segments of the population.

Kissing up is being kind, showing respect while taking initiative. Yes, the sisters had an agenda. Yes, they wanted something for themselves and their children. Yes, they knew they were in a limited box within which they had to operate. Instead of kicking against the box, they worked within it and found ways to expand their boundaries. In a way, they understood the prayer of Jabez to "enlarge their territory" without causing harm to anyone: *"Oh, that You would bless me indeed, and enlarge my territory, that Your hand would be with me, and that You would keep me from evil, that I may not cause pain!"*[8]

You can make a move up by kissing up without turning people off or putting people down. You don't have to step on or over someone in order to move up. Instead, be kind, respectful, and assertive instead of aggressive. In pastoral counseling, we learned about being aggressive, assertive, passive, and passive-aggressive. The most positive way to take the initiative is by being assertive. Know who you are, your limits and strengths. Decide to take an initiative to connect with others even when they don't want a relationship with you. Make a plan, a good one, one that blesses others as well as yourself, and then kiss up.

You can make a move that might get you ostracized. Don't let the fear of striking out keep you from swinging the bat. Start up and kiss up. You can't move up without initiative. You might make a move that will shut more doors than open them for you if you don't learn the kissing up principle.

Five Keys for Kissing Up Right!

Let's get very practical at this point. I want to help you go to the next level. The daughters of Zelophehad needed something. If they had been into women's rights, we might have said that they were being denied their rights and that they had every right to protest. But they chose a kinder, gentler, but assertive rather than aggressive approach. They kissed up.

Key 1. Kissing up recognizes and respects the authority of those who have the power to give you what you need. I am advocating a respect for the office or position of the person in authority. Every profession and vocation has key people who are instrumental to your achievement, advancement, and success. Contrary to popular belief, you cannot make it alone. Some call it connecting or networking; I call it kissing up. While the person you need to kiss up to will certainly have flaws and weaknesses, you must see beyond the person to the position. Whether you like the person or not isn't particularly relevant. They can give you what you need if you decide to be kind instead of foolish.

Key 2. Kissing up often requires an attitude change. The truth is that Jesus adopted an attitude unbefitting a king or lord. He humbled himself, became a servant and died to make a point, implement a plan, and execute His agenda.[9] Humility is the taproot of kindness.

Key 3. Kissing up makes a good, workable plan to connect positively with the right people in the right way so that you receive what you need instead of taking or seizing it. Proceed with a godly and good plan to move up. Pray. Listen to the counsel of a multitude of wise people. I have five elders in my life I run things past at various times, to seek their wisdom. Be creative. Think outside the box. Use tradition as a key to open doors without becoming a slave to tradition. When you break man's rules, understand that there may be painful consequences but know that short-term pain can often bring long-term gain. Stop complaining about today's pain; focus on tomorrow's gain. Keep focused and don't be distracted. Work the plan even when you can't see the end results. Those who invest wisely and prudently in the stock market often go through bull markets that inflict significant losses on their portfolios, but they know that if they can weather the storm, they will see long-term profits that will overcome the short-term losses.

Key 4. Kissing up takes the initiative to kindly connect with others. When rejected, the initiator continues for weeks, months, or years to practice the Golden Rule and thereby win a friend instead of defeating an enemy. This takes seriously the words of Jesus, "Use your worldly resources to benefit others and make friends. In this way, your generosity stores up a reward for you in heaven."[10]

Key 5. Kissing up refuses to give up. In others words, connecting with others to create a mutual blessing doesn't depend on their response. Your unilateral initiative of kindness is unconditional. Their rejection doesn't prompt you to withdraw or give up.

Are you ready for an attitude change? Give up your self-centered pride and replace it with selfless serving and humility. Replace the take-no-prisoners mentality with kindness. Decide to move up by kissing *up!*

Kiss *Up* Steps

- Connect kindly with people who can help you move up by kissing up.
- Respect the office of the person in authority as you kiss up.
- Don't allow rejection to cause you to give up.
- Seek wise counsel of those you feel are credible and have your best interests in mind.
- Remember to plan wisely before you initiate connecting with people.
- Refuse to compromise who you are or your values when kissing up.
- Take the initiative to connect with those whom you will bless and who will bless you. Understand that you are blessed to be a blessing to others seeking to kiss up to you!

CHAPTER 6

Listen Up! ---------------------------------

To everything there is a season,
A time for every purpose under heaven:
A time to be born, and a time to die;
A time to plant, and a time to pluck what is planted;
A time to kill, and a time to heal;
A time to break down, and a time to build up;
A time to weep, and a time to laugh;
A time to mourn, and a time to dance;
A time to cast away stones, and a time to gather stones;
A time to embrace, and a time to refrain from embracing;
A time to gain, and a time to lose;
A time to keep, and a time to throw away;
A time to tear, and a time to sew;
A time to keep silence, and a time to speak;
A time to love, and a time to hate;
A time of war, and a time of peace.[1]

There's a time for speaking and there's also a time for listening. Ecclesiastes tells us there's a time for everything under the heavens. At times you must be still and hear God. With the hurriedness of life and the rushed, stressed, and busy society we live in today, we often miss the subtle messages.

I believe that's why God spoke the way He did to Elijah in the cave. Elijah had been waiting. He'd been running from Queen Jezebel, who wanted to kill him. So hiding in a cave he was waiting for God to speak. Wind, an earthquake, and fire came. God didn't speak through any of those. Then came a still, small voice. Only when Elijah stopped running and refused to be caught up in natural distractions did he hear the still, small voice of God.

> The LORD said, "Go out and stand on the mountain in the presence of the LORD, for the LORD is about to pass by."

> Then a great and powerful wind tore the mountains apart and shattered the rocks before the LORD, but the LORD was not in the wind. After the wind there was an earthquake, but the LORD was not in the earthquake. After the earthquake came a fire, but the LORD was not in the fire. And after the fire came a gentle whisper. When Elijah heard it, he pulled his cloak over his face and went out and stood at the mouth of the cave.

Then a voice said to him, "What are you doing here, Elijah?"[2]

Listening up is learning to take the time to hear that still, small voice and to know the voice of God. In John 10, Jesus says that his sheep know his voice. When Jesus speaks, we listen. Where he leads, we follow. And one of the places he leads us is by still waters. I love the comfort of Psalm 23, "The Lord is my shepherd, I shall not want. He makes me to lie down in green pastures. He leads me beside still waters. He restores my soul." Listening to the shepherd will bring us to a place of rest.

Take a Sabbatical

What you want to begin to do is to have a sabbatical. The word *sabbatical* comes from the Hebrew word for Sabbath which means "rest." I'm talking here about a vacation! A vacation, a Sabbath for the soul, which means I vacate the premises and I go to a place where I can hear myself and my God. Recreation means re-creation. I leave the place where I am spending all my time and energy, and I am re-created and replenished from that which I have poured out to others and for others. What I have given is now restored to me. In those moments when I am led by the still waters and my soul is restored then I can hear God. My Creator is continually renewing and re-creating me. I must take the time and grant my Creator permission to build me up and edify me.

I must hear God so I can make the moves necessary for my life and for the lives that I affect. We touch many lives and we influence many lives, and if we go in with a tired, hurried, nonlistening posture we will make bad decisions and irritate a whole lot of folks.

So I encourage you to start listening. Be intentional about it. Personally, I'm trying to live a life that pleases God. So I pray, "God, I do not want to do anything in life that is not in your perfect will." But if I don't listen to Him, how can I know His perfect will? Recently I went through Holy Week and I conducted seven worship services. In six of them, I was preaching. It was difficult for me to squeeze everything in—worship, family, work, and sleep. So, instead of being a Holy Week, it was a harried week. I had crammed and planned far too much into one seven-day period. Even God rested one out of seven days.

I know these special Easter services come every year. I should have planned and rested up for them . . . but instead I found myself very fatigued as Holy Week approached. So, I actually took some days off and I didn't go to the office. I would just lie down before the Lord each day and rest. As I napped and rested, the message I needed to preach would come to me. I would get the points for the sermon for that day's service. In that time of rest and listening, the Scripture "In Him we live, move, and have our very being"[3] became true for me.

God took my tired body because I was willing to listen and hear and He gave me a fresh anointing to preach. All seven services of Holy Week were unquestionably blessed. I was able to listen to God as I rested. I kept a pad by my bed and I wrote every word down. I would encourage everyone to keep a pad and pen by their bed and in a pocket or purse where it is easily accessible so when God begins to speak, what He says can be written down. You may not hear everything God has to say to you all at once. But take the words, phrases, and sentences that God speaks to your heart and write them down. As time passes those nuggets and individual pieces will begin to fit together like puzzle pieces and the vision or dream that God has for you will become visible.

I had a battle once and this happens when people are moving up. You are going to encounter battles along the way as you are moving up. This happens to every leader or mover. In I Chronicles 20 Jehoshaphat, for example, had four different groups of people telling him things and giving him advice. So he called a fast and began fasting and praying so he could hear what God had to say. God spoke in the midst of the congregation and raised up a man to speak. Every time there's a crisis God says, "I don't want you to be in a moving active state; I want you to be in a listening posture." One of my fathers in the faith declares that just as we offer one tenth of every dollar (the tithe) to the Lord, we should set aside at least one out of every ten days for a "listening/consecration day for God," and do nothing but lay in God's presence. It is to get into a listening mode. No phones. No TV. Just you and God.

Listening Empowers You to Go Through Life's Battles

Years ago, as a young pastor, I had to learn to *listen up*. A situation arose that I didn't know how to handle. It came from left field, it came from my inner circle, and it came from people I would never have expected it to come from. I experienced a Judas betrayal from a person close to me, and I said to God, "I don't know how to handle this."

In the middle of the night, God would wake me up. I would have my pad by the bed and God would give me the step for the next day. He wouldn't give me a week's worth of steps—only the next step. When we speak the Lord's prayer, we petition, "Give us *this* day our daily bread." In Psalms we read, "Your word is a lamp to my feet and a light to my path."[4] Walking is taking one step at a time. We don't need light for the whole journey all at once. We only need a word for the next step. That's what God was giving to me.

He gave me the step for the next day of how to handle particular people and how to kiss up to certain people. This time of listening to God and taking just a step at a time lasted for about a month. Then, the victory was won; the strongholds and the walls were down. God's blessing came through all the difficulties I was experiencing. I listened to the Lord and He led me through the valley of darkness that I had to walk through.

Stay in a listening posture. You can successfully go through trials and difficulties by listening to God. You must take time to rest and to hear, and when you do, God will speak. The question is, *will you listen?* In the Old Testament, Isaiah 6:8, the prophet responds to God's question, "Who will go for us and whom shall I send?" And Isaiah responds, "Here am I, send me." It's not that God wasn't speaking all the time; it's just that Isaiah had finally taken the time to listen. And it's interesting because he did not hear God until King Uzziah, whose life Isaiah had been very intricately with, died. Who or what do you need to move out of your life in order to hear God more clearly?

Listen Up Communicates Caring

Each up has its own set of virtues. What virtue does listening communicate? Simply this: *caring*. Listening communicates a sense of caring and concern for the other person. In fact, listening is one of the most significant gifts you can give to others. Listening says to the other person:

- "I care."
- "I am here, present, and attentive to you."
- "I want to hear and understand you."
- "I am spending time with you."
- "I think you and what you say are important."
- "I want to share with you."

Listening is both a virtue and a skill. The skill of listening up includes these important techniques:

1. **Paraphrasing**. When you listen, seek to understand and then speak back to the person what you are hearing. Say something like, "Let me be sure I understand you. I heard you say [repeat what you heard]. Is that right?" And then let them correct and affirm what you heard to verify that you heard that person correctly.

2. **Reflecting feelings**. Also pick up on nonverbal com-

munication. Notice the person's facial expression, tone of voice, body language, appearance, eye contact or lack of it, willingness to touch or be touched, etc. In other words, what people don't say but communicate nonverbally is as important as what they do say with words. Reflect back to that person who is talking the feelings that you perceive such as joy or sadness, grief or relief, anger or forgiveness, and so forth.

3. **Affirming and accepting**. Listening up affirms others. They feel your warmth, acceptance, and affirmation when you are willing to listen to them and truly try to understand their feelings. Scripturally, we accept one another as the Lord has accepted us.[5] Acceptance doesn't mean you agree with their statements or beliefs. Rather, listening communicates that you accept the other person as a person of worth, dignity, and importance.

4. **Self-disclosing**. Share from your heart. Be transparent. As the other person shares their feelings and thoughts honestly, be open and honest with them. Don't judge and condemn. Rather, identify and validate their feelings as honestly as you can without compromising truth. Instead of saying, "I know how you feel," say instead, "At times, I have felt that way when I experienced ———."

5. **Describing behavior**. Let them know how they are coming across with their works and actions. Describe to

them how their actions impact yourself and others. Be a mirror for them. A good listener helps others see themselves as others see them.

Listening up isn't becoming a garbage can for the negative thoughts and feelings of others. At times, my children will tell me how terrible a teacher, parent, or coach is. They dump their negative feelings on me. If I'm not careful, I will receive their junk without questioning the validity of their judgments. Then, the next time I see that adult, I will find myself owning those negative feelings. Sure, my children felt better after they had dumped on me, but then I felt miserable, frustrated, or angry. When others want you to listen simply to use you as a garbage can for their negativity, tug on your earlobe and say to them, "This is an ear, not a garbage can. I refuse to listen to your garbage. Don't dump on me. I can't take responsibility for your feelings. Don't blame others or me for the way you feel. You choose to feel the way you do. Take responsibility for your own feelings!"

Listening up is about debriefing not dumping. Just as you don't have to be anyone's doormat, you also don't have to be their trash can. Debriefing helps the other person do reality testing and sort through their feelings without you agreeing or taking responsibility for them. Debriefing speaks the truth in love to another person.[6]

Listening up is a valuable gift you give to another person of your time and attention. Don't let others abuse that gift. Set boundaries. At times you will have to say, "I choose not to listen to that," when the input is gossip, libelous, slanderous, backbiting, abusive, or offensive. Marriage, friendship, or being related isn't a free ticket for abusive dumping. You may have people in your life that call and drain you. When you need to rest and refresh, turn the phone, beeper, or e-mail off or just don't answer. Go to a quiet, secret place, to commune with God and be renewed. Encourage yourself in the Lord. Develop a support network of people who will listen to you.

Again, the virtue of listening up is caring. When you give of your time and attention to another person, you communicate that you care. What a powerful gift listening up will be in maturing and growing your relationships with others and God.

Remember that prayer, a form of listening up, is not just telling God about what you want. It's also listening to God for what He wants; God has wonderful plans for your life if you will just *listen up!*

Are You Willing to Stop and Listen?

Down in the hills of North Carolina, we used to go to vacation Bible school and sing this song, "In the Garden":

I come to the garden alone
While the dew is still on the roses
And the voice I hear, falling on my ear
The Son of God discloses

And He walks with me
And He talks with me
And He tells me I am His own
And the joy we share as we tarry there
None other has ever known

He speaks and the sound of His voice
Is so sweet the birds hush their singing
And the melody that He gave to me
Within my heart is ringing

And He walks with me
And He talks with me
And He tells me I am His own

And the joy we share as we tarry there
None other has ever known[7]

Listening is going alone to that garden. The great thing about listening to God is you don't need a group. Nobody else needs to know what you are doing or when you're doing it. You can come to the garden alone and God will minister to your inner spirit.

You don't need to go to or through anyone to get to God. God is only a prayer away.

Be Quick to Listen and Slow to Speak

1 Timothy 1:9 reads, "Be quick to listen, slow to speak, slow to anger." We are in such a verbal society. We're in the midst of verbal campaigns, geared to outspeak and outdo the other person. The most quick-witted one is the one who will get the most votes. But there is an art to speaking and there's an art to knowing when to speak up. "Being slow to speak" means processing and taking things in, listening, really understanding what is being said before you speak.

Decide if you are the one who is to speak or not. I have often said and written in my books, "Not every battle is your battle." You have to choose what you're going to say and also choose what situations you're going to insert yourself into. Choose wisely. Deborah, the first female judge and prophetess of Israel understood this well (Judges 4) and did not go to battle with Sisera until she was sure this was the battle God would have her enter. Has someone come to you and asked for your help on something you are not feeling comfortable with in your spirit? Well, my dear, then it's listening time. The world calls it intuition, but God calls it the Holy Spirit and it speaks to our inner self and teaches us truth.[8] One of my friends says "Follow that *first* voice."

The daughters of Zelophehad did not move hastily. They had a strategy in mind. That's why they went through all those steps like talking to Moses, going to the priests, then the elders and then to the congregation. Each step was necessary. As they walked through their journey one step at a time, they were gathering information. They didn't move as soon as they talked to Moses, that's not how the story went. But the text also says that they stood by the door of the tabernacle—that is the sanctuary, the altar, where we meet and greet God. They were gathering information because they were setting up a strategy. They were determining if they had enough and if the timing was right to be able to come before the leaders in authority to ask for an upgrade, to ask for promotion, to ask for a set of laws to be changed.

When you're moving up you're saying, "I'm not comfortable anymore being in this place at this time in this way." You may be saying to yourself, "I've done my thirty years. I've gotten the gold watch. I need something more than the window at the post office" or "I need something more than the changing of diapers." So when I'm talking about moving up, I'm talking about honoring the resources that God has placed in your hands. I can't speak until I know what those resources are and what He wants me to do with them.

So, the text says be slow to open your mouth, be slow in what you're going to speak about. The daughters of Zelophehad looked at the situation. There's a verse here that is very important in their strategy: "Our father died in the desert, He was not among Korah's followers, who banded together against the Lord, but he died for his own sin and left no sons." In other words, "Our daddy did not die as the others did in the wilderness. He didn't go against God. The others had rebelled against God and they clearly had God's wrath on them. But our daddy died because it was his time, in dying, he left no sons." What they were doing was processing the facts to make the distinction of how and why their dad, and they as his descendants, needed to be honored. These sisters were excellent examples of how to be *slow to speak*—process, observe, and honor; *quick to listen*—take in what God, Moses, and the leaders had to say; and *slow to anger*—they didn't explode in rage when they first didn't receive what was rightfully theirs.

Being quick to listen and slow to speak is a gift you can give others. One of the greatest gifts you can give another person is taking the time to listen and to understand what they are saying. Don't interrupt. Refuse to inject your opinions before you have fully heard and understood theirs. Be patient. Don't let angry feelings prompt you to cut off communication or to say something now that you will regret later. Listen up!

We can learn from Zelophehad's daughters to check out the process, to wait and be clear that this is our time to speak, that it is our turn to speak and our battle to wage with God. When you do, you'll have an outcome like they did. As you move up, decide to listen up. Listen well to God and to the wise counsel of others. Decide now that your first response will not be an angry outburst even if you feel it's justified. Instead, move up as you listen *up*!

Listen *Up* Steps

- Keep a pad and pen close by you at all times so that you can listen to God and jot down what He speaks to you.

- Take a sabbatical rest. It may be for a day, or weeks, or months. You may need a vacation in order to get away from the bustle and hear God.

- Take a crisis one step at a time. Listen to God for guidance about each step you should take.

- Be quick to listen, slow to speak, and slow to anger. Seek to hear and understand before you respond.

CHAPTER 7

Hang Up!

To everything there is a season. That goes for associates as well. Ever received a phone call you didn't want to take and that lasted far longer than you wanted to listen? What you needed to do was simply hang *up*! Hang up means that there is a clear beginning and a clear end to your season for that relationship. As you end a season, you need to look at the people with whom you hang. Some people work good for your life in a particular season, but they do not grow or go with you into the next season. The good fruit of the previous season hangs around too long and spoils.

I was on the phone with a friend who had made a decision to move on from his job but was allowing himself to take calls from the old place so that he began to doubt his decision to move. He needed to hang up on the old and move into the new. Some people cannot go with you into the new thing. Kindly but persistently, hang up.

The kids that I went to kindergarten and first grade with were wonderful for that time of my life, we were playmates. However, when I entered a private country school and we moved out of the neighborhood, I was entering a new season. We moved away from all that we knew, but we also moved to a new expansion of the resources and opportunities for the next season of life. So some of the friends I had in the first and second grade would not be my seventh- and eighth-grade friends. I was developing a new season and hanging up on the old.

Hanging up means it's time to shore up boundaries. You have to put out of your life, or abstain from them gracefully and assertively, the people who are no longer good for this new season in which you find yourself. In Isaiah, God says, "Do not consider the former things nor consider the things of old. Behold I will do a new thing, now it shall spring forth."[1] You are to walk in the newness, which means you must let go of past negatives— ideas, people, and feelings. You cannot accept negatives. As you enter this new season there are those who will not see why you're doing what you're doing. You can't accept negatives via e-mail, text messages, blogs, MySpace, or phone. That season is over and you are not to feel guilty about it. It's often said that "two negatives make a positive." I would suggest that you make a positive by eliminating two negative people and moving them out of your life.

If others begin to burden and bog you down, you have to release them. You need to be able to hang up on them. Press the delete key on the e-mail. Use your caller ID. You must physically and emotionally separate from those who would put you into bondage. When that phone call comes that you don't need to be part of, you need to be able to find a way to say, "No more. Thank you but I'm not in your control any longer." Hang up. It's not being rude; it's protecting yourself from hurt, harm, and the danger of retreating back to where God has just delivered you from!

How to Hang Up

How do you hang up on people? Well, it's called developing savvy, seasoning, and knowing when it is your time to move on and up. Some of it happens naturally. One way is to stop accepting some appointments. Realize you have a choice. Remember, No is a complete sentence, "No, thank you," if you want to be polite. But you do not have to go to the family reunion any longer if every time you go in the room they are joking about you and what you are now doing. Maybe they used to tease you as a freckled little red-haired girl when you were in third grade but now you're thirty and their comments are not funny or cute (if they ever were). You're trying to find a season of your life. So you may make a decision this year not to go to the family reunion. You may decide to sow your time into something that will bring you fulfillment. Learn to hang up.

For example, I was tired of old Fourth of July parties. My girlfriends and I decided that none of us were going to go to the typical backyard barbeque that we've been going to for thirtysome years. Instead, we were going to a jazz festival in New Orleans with some amazing artists and enjoying some new, phenomenal friends. For six months we planned. We got our tickets and rooms and moved up to a new thing for July Fourth. I had developed a new set of activities with new friends. I was hanging up on the old and welcoming in the new.

Something fresh needs to happen. Hanging up is never easy. Letting go of the past that had weighed you down and seizing the new that will move you up requires the courage to change. One of the nuances behind *chadash,* the Hebrew word for *new,* is "change, fresh." It's time for a breath of fresh air in your life. A fresh wind needs to blow out the stale, putrid air in the areas of your past relationships that have become negative and draining. In Italian, it is *la vida nuovo dulce*—the sweet new life. Life does not have to be so hard all the time; it really can be sweet. Moving up is sweet.

Something new requiring change is around the corner.
Around the corner from enslaving relationships that
dominated, intimated, and manipulated you are new
friends who respect and honor you, encourage and edify
you, and who believe that your past doesn't dictate your
future. The change that needs to happen will begin in
you. Stop praying for God to change those negative people around you; start praying for God to change you.
They may continually resist change, but you're ready for
it. Change requires courage. The courage to let go of old,
stifling securities and to grasp new, exciting possibilities.

The daughters of Zelophehad were moving into a
new realm. No one in their culture had considered such
a bold request before. No women had asked for what
had been reserved only for men in the past. They chal-
lenged the existing system. They sought change in order
to move up into a future that would include them and
their offspring instead of neglecting and ignoring them.
They had to hang up on fear and timidity. These sisters
refused to go to family or friends who might discourage,
distract, or disappoint them. Any person who would
challenge the greatest ruler of the day, like Moses had in
confronting the Egyptian pharaoh, would certainly be
open to a new thing from God. These women hung up
on past tradition and possible naysayers and took their
request to a possibility thinker—Moses. They also

trusted that Moses would listen to God and not just men. They discerned correctly.

Hanging up is about creating new scenarios that will fulfill your dreams. In the workforce, it's about targeting and attending continuing education events, conferences, and conventions that will support the moving up in your life surrounding yourself with possible thinkers. Invest in yourself!

For example, when people I coach who say they want to be professional speakers, if it's just on a local level that they want to speak, like at their job or for work-related presentations, I'll direct them in a different manner to classes or groups that can help. But if they say, "I like what you do and I want to go on the road and make my living speaking," I introduce them to Toastmasters or the National Speakers Association. I say to them, "Well you know that the convention for the National Speakers is coming up, so instead of being at the normal barbeque on the holiday weekend, you may need to be at the National Speakers Association where you can develop new friends and colleagues who will benefit your moving up." To move up you have to strategically choose ways to advance and people and places that enhance.

Boundaries are necessary. Begin with new boundaries. It's a matter of putting in boundaries where necessary, creating new experiences that bring you fulfillment, and associating with people who are like-minded. Boundaries mean, "I love myself and must protect myself." I have boundaries for myself, my family, my office hours, my sleeping hours. I know what I need to function adequately and to maintain my quality of life. My family takes priority, so I must insert them in my own life. I am now in a season of raising teenagers and that is a very different season than just a few years ago. My office hours, my travel, and my down time all have had to shift for this new season.

Some of your old friends may say, "I don't like that music." "Okay, well you won't be going with us to the jazz festival in New Orleans then and that's fine. I release you to pursue your own fulfillment." This is what I tell my congregation to say when they come up against a person who's really not receiving them well, "I release you to your new season. Please release me to mine."

Some of your old friends are lazy, crazy, or both. What do I mean? Lazy are those people who have no purpose or goals in life. They are a drag on you and are going nowhere themselves. They complain and criticize but never change or move up. Ask yourself, "What are they doing for God, themselves, or others?" The answer will be, Nothing!

Then there are the crazy folks. Such people have irrational beliefs. They keep doing the same thing the same old way and expecting something to change. They refuse to accept the truths of God and keep believing the myths of others or the lies from their past unhealthy relationships.

A wise and profitable lesson can be learned from the story of Jesus and the paralytic man at the Pool of Bethesda.[2] For thirty-eight years, this paralytic had hung around sick and infirm folks never hearing from anyone that he or they had the potential or possibility of walking. Sometimes, an angel would stir the water and the first person in the water would be healed. No one ever helped this man so he could never get into the water first.

Then Jesus came through and asked the lame man, "Do you want to be well?" What a crazy question! The lame man complained and protested that no one ever would help him into the water. Jesus refused to listen to the excuses or complaints. He simply issued a command, "Rise, take up your bed and walk." Some action is required on your part; this is something no one else can do for you. You alone must act!

Get up and move on. What is it you need to rise to? What must you "take up." You, like the healed man, may need to take up your bed and walk away. You don't need any reminders of where you've been and what you've been doing for years in that same position. That takes you down. To rise is an up movement. You can't allow the crazy people in life—complainers, irrational thinkers, blamers, haters, and negative thinkers—to tell you what's possible. They've resigned themselves to the fact that all you will ever be is what you've been. The truth is, you can change. God's new thing for you is just around the corner. Something fresh is blowing in the wind.

There are also lazy people around that pool who really don't have any goals, who are not going to motivate you and may not even know how to because they haven't motivated themselves. So you have them as just another boundary. You must decide if you have the time or energy to be around such lazy and crazy people. Only after you hang up will you move up. As you move into a new season with movers and shakers you must hang up on the lazys and crazys.

Another thing is important to understand. The crazy people from your past will never understand where you are going. As you grow and the Lord elevates you, they will become very emotionally unstable or jealous about it. Sometimes it's in your own family and you don't even see it until it happens. I experienced this scenario when my mother died. There were some people who had been very close to me and my mother for years and had even attended my services. Along with my mom, I felt they were very excited for me and they were kind of like my cheerleaders. But when my mother was dying all kinds of insecurities came out. They began to say things like, "We never liked what you were doing all along."

I had to make a decision; it was a very difficult moment for me. I came to realize that they really didn't have my best interests at heart. I had to decide not to allow the crazy elements, the insecurities in their lives, to destabilize and unsettle me. I had to say to some of them, "We're going to remain in relationship but not fellowship: it does not mean I have to spend a lot of time with you. So for this particular season in my life, I release you to get the help that you need or to be with people of like-mindedness that you want to be around. But one thing is clear for me, I can't be around you right now."

Get Real . . . Be Honest with Yourself and Others

What's so refreshing to me in relationships are people who are just real and honest with me. Hanging up requires the virtue of honesty and the ability to accept reality. Why hang on to a relationship when it's really over? Why continue in a job that makes you and others miserable? Why maintain a friendship that hangs you out to dry?

Hanging up requires you to get real, get over it, and get beyond it by being honest. What's virtuous about honesty is that it faces the truth and chooses to act upon truth instead of procrastinating, denying, or rationalizing. The truth may be painful but continuing on in denial will ultimately cause more pain and destruction in you and others. How does honesty help you hang up? Here are the steps to facing up to the facts and confronting the truth in preparation for hanging up.

- **Face the facts**. Stop denying what's happening to you and the other person. The relationship is going nowhere and instead of blessing both of you, it's draining and paining you both.
- **Get wise counsel**. Wisdom comes from a multitude of counselors.[3] Receive wise counsel from people around you who love you enough to tell you the truth instead of what they think you want to hear. Counselors, pastors, mentors, and teachers have wisdom, knowledge, understanding, and experience that can help you if you will listen. Seeking their counsel isn't a sign of weakness; it's a manifestation of inner strength and courage. Do reality testing with them. Bounce your thoughts and feelings off of them to test what's real versus what's simply your private and peculiar perception.
- **Pray**. Ask God's Spirit to help and guide you. After all, God's Spirit is named the counselor, comforter, interpreter, and helper.[4] Remember that

God sees beyond the horizon of your limited vision. God has already been where you're going. I've heard some say, "I don't know what tomorrow holds, but I know the One who holds tomorrow." Trust God when he says to you, " 'For I know the plans I have for you,' declares the LORD, 'plans to prosper you and not to harm you, plans to give you hope and a future.' "[5]

- **Take action**. Once you get the big thoughts that are true and reality based from God and others, you must execute, that is, take action. The authors of *Execution: The Discipline of Getting Things Done* comment, "Unless you translate big thoughts into concrete steps for action, they're pointless. Without execution, the breakthrough thinking breaks down, learning adds no value, people don't meet their stretch goals, and the revolution stops dead in its tracks."[6]

It's Time to Hang Up and Prosper

Consider the words of Psalm 1:

Oh, the joys of those
who do not follow the advice of the wicked,

or stand around with sinners,
or join in with scoffers.
But they delight in doing everything the LORD wants;
day and night they think about his law.
They are like trees planted along the riverbank,
bearing fruit each season without fail.
Their leaves never wither
and in all they do, they prosper.[7]

You're supposed to prosper and not wither; so figure out what kind of trees you are hanging around or that you were planted around by your parents or previous associates. Don't hang around people who are evil, complaining, blaming, mocking, or simply negative about everything. Don't sow seeds where you've been planted near bad soil or weeds. Weed your garden and prune your plants. Ask yourself, *Is this person bearing good fruit?* This question is one I use regarding our interns coming through our church, particularly since we are a training ground for women in ministry. They want to be near me and be with me since I am seen as a mentor for women. But I find that many of them come in just to observe, not to get involved or become accountable. They are lazy and slow and expecting me to do the work for them. They just want to show up on Sunday.

Well, for me that's part of the lazy crew. They want

the gravy but they have not put any meat on the stove and have not done anything to produce it. They want my drippings but they're not willing to create their own. So what I'm saying is that you have to be around people with a work ethic, with integrity, and stay away from people who don't exhibit these traits because it will affect you.

When Is It Time to Hang Up?

So, hang up when you find yourself repeatedly unhappy, unfulfilled, tossing and turning at night, leaving a place and saying, "Why do I feel bad every time I leave here?" It's that type of feeling. That's why you need to be in tune with yourself. The Bible talks about the brothers of Issachar, who were able to discern the time. "From the tribe of Issachar, there were 200 leaders of the tribe with their relatives. All these men understood the temper of the times and knew the best course for Israel to take."[8] We have people in the world who think they have a sixth sense but there is a timing in God, and we can know it.

For example, we know when it's time to eat. We know when it's time to drink. You know God has created you with a biological clock. We know that everything in the universe is divinely designed and timed. So in nine months, babies have to come out. They can't be carried anymore. Relationships have "time" also. We can also know when a relationship has gone as far as it can go and it's time to release it. It's the same thing with our experiences. You know when the time is up. It's a matter of whether you are bold enough and courageous enough to say, "I've had enough." Or to declare, "This isn't working anymore," and it's time to hang up. As my kids say, "I'm not feeling this anymore."

Some relationships are all give and no return. Some people want to use you, manipulate you, control you, or intimidate you. That's a toxic relationship to you and you need to hang up on toxic relationships. For example, I may have a business relationship that has come to the end of its prosperous season for both of us. That relationship cannot continue to the next level for one or both of us. I have to make a decision: Is this where we stop our business relationship and maintain our personal one? Will we be able to end part of it without hurting each other? Here's where the speak up principle comes into play. I need to speak up and tell that person that the business portion or our relationship has gone to the highest level that we can go to together. I need to hang up that part of our relationship.

There is a biblical example of a similar situation

where Paul and Silas had been working together success-fully for Jesus. They had been a powerful team. But for the next planned trip, they were not the team and they were not going together. Sometimes I watch *The Apprentice* with my children, and we learn some impor-tant business principles from it. One thing we have seen is that when it gets down to the wire, people are not usu-ally with the same team they started out with. I've watched as they have become distracted from the mission because of a toxic relationship. A few of them got angry with each other so they couldn't work together any longer. Teams get moved around because they are not effective staying with the group they came in. They may have come in all excited and wanting to work together, but now they end up getting in each other's way.

Well, in life you have the same kind of timing, but you don't have Hollywood experts or a Mr. Trump stand-ing there saying, "It's time to change the teams around." You do, however, have the Holy Spirit in you who says, "How many more times are you going to let that man hit you? Are you going to continue to let that person abuse you? How long are you going to let that job deflate your spirit? How much is that worth? Is getting six figures worth getting heartburn every night?"

You have to really listen up—to yourself and to

God—for the time to say, "It's time to hang this one up." Setting boundaries, moving on from toxic relationships, deciding to change, and releasing old patterns and bad habits while learning new and constructive ones requires courage, work, and commitment. This chapter may be really prompting you to take action. Let me help you make a decision now. Hang *up!*

Steps to Hang *Up*

- Discern the toxic relationships in your life and move toward a time and season for hanging up.

- Hang up when the relationship is controlling, manipulative, intimidating, abusive, or addictive.

- Prepare yourself to hang up by praying, seeking wise counsel, facing the facts, and taking action.

- Refuse to associate with blaming, critical, and judgmental people.

- Cut yourself off from evil, wicked, and mocking relationships.

- Set healthy boundaries, refusing to relate to people who tear you down instead of build you up.

- Move up to positive, prosperous healthy relationships after you hang up on the old and embrace God's new for your life.

- Decide how long you want your cell phone on each day and use your caller ID. I have a rule for a certain time to shut it down. This is family time or my time.

CHAPTER 8

Make Up! ---------------------------------

Forgiveness, forgiveness, forgiveness is so crucial in all the areas of our lives. One of the reasons so many of us are physically sick is because disease means we are at dis-ease, out of ease with ourselves and others. It's akin to a car out of alignment or a joint out of place. We function, but not at the maximum level for which we were intended. The body is the temple of the Holy Spirit, the Scriptures tell us. Therefore, the body needs to reflect wholeness and love, attributes of God, and be in alignment with itself. The lack of forgiveness is one of the greatest destroyers of humans because we do have conflicts and bruised feelings that get bottled up inside of us and must be released. Often, we blast others with anger and frustration allowing walls of unforgiveness to go up.

We need to be slow to speak, slow to anger, and quick to listen.[1] We do have powerful emotions, and if we allow them to become pent up inside of us, all of our repressed negative emotions will have to go somewhere. So, unforgiveness begins to manifest itself physically and emotionally while creating a multitude of disease symptoms in our bodies and souls.

I have to be ready to say, I am willing to be liberated. I am willing to get myself out of this knot I'm tied in because I can't go forward when I'm balled up with this knot of unforgiveness. So I am making a decision like Jesus did that I am going to forgive even when I wasn't at fault. I'm taking the high ground, walking the high road. I know that for things to go forward, I've got to be free. But if I don't forgive, I am not free.

Refuse to Stay Offended

Jesus speaks of being offended this way:

> Then He said to the disciples, "It is impossible that no offense should come, but woe to him through whom they do come! It would be better for him if a millstone were hung around his neck, and he were thrown into the sea, than that he should offend one of these little ones. Take heed to yourselves. If your brother sins against you, rebuke him; and if he repents, forgive him. And if he sins against you seven times in a day, and seven times in a day returns to you, saying, 'I repent,' you shall forgive him."[2]

In *The Bait of Satan,* John Brevere describes an offense as bait in a trap. "The Greek word for 'offend' in Luke 17:1 comes from the word *skandalon.* This word originally referred to the part of the trap to which the bait was attached. Hence the word signifies laying a trap in someone's way."[3] Becoming offended and choosing not to forgive others traps us in a destructive cycle of anger, blame, alienation, and isolation.

I have seen families use the trap of offense in not forgiving a family member and using children as pawns. They keep grandchildren away from grandparents or siblings apart from one another as a way to hurt, manipulate, and alienate one another. Families are torn apart by offense, unforgiveness, and anger. The wall of unresolved anger becomes a barrier in marriages and families causing divorce, separation, and hurt that can last for generations.

Don't Take the Bait

When we are tempted by the bait of offense and take it, we find ourselves trapped with unforgiveness and mired in bitterness. A root of bitterness begins to form in our hearts and we discover that we are unable to form trusting, loving relationships with others and with God.

How do we move up toward God by making up, forgiving one another? Scripture poses this question in a number of ways: "How can we say we love God whom we cannot see, when we cannot love our neighbor whom we see everyday?"

Refuse to be offended. The temptation to be offended always seems to be presenting itself. At times, people intentionally hurt us and we must decide whether to be offended or to forgive, even if they don't ask for forgiveness. Here's a positive attitude: *Choose to forgive before they repent. Choose to forgive even if they don't repent.* That takes the weight off of you and allows your flow to continue. The person an offense really hurts is the person choosing to be offended. If we wait until another person repents or asks for forgiveness, we become a slave to our own negative feelings and actions. We must choose to forgive unconditionally—no strings attached, no grudges held—in order to be set free from the bondage of an offended attitude.

Release your angry feelings to God, not onto others. One by one begin to release those offending situations and hurtful people. Forgive, whether you say it verbally to that person or do it in your own heart. A good way to start is to sit down and start writing down what you are angry about. If this is not dealt with in alienated families, offense can last for years. People go without speaking or making contact. Pray. Ask God to give you the power to let go of unforgiveness and to reach out in loving forgiveness to others. Remember that many offenses are unintentional. You became upset with another person, but they never intended to hurt you or cause you pain. Your expectations were unfulfilled or your unrealistic needs went unmet, and you snatched the bait of offense. In this case, you need to examine yourself.

The New Testament also teaches us not to go to bed on our anger.[4] How much wisdom is contained in this thought! While we are asleep, activity is still going on. It needs to be positive energy so that it will manifest in positive and good feelings for the next day. I have even made it a practice not to watch the late TV news, so that my subconscious will not be working on the negative, but on the positive. Instead, I make a list of good things to reflect upon; positive experiences from the day and things I am looking forward to in the next.

Examine yourself. Often if you ask offended people what started all the anger, hurt, and pain, they have forgotten the original cause. Some families have carried on feuds for generations and the ones who began it are long gone or are very old. There is *no* need to carry intergenerational unforgiveness. What are the lessons we are teaching our children? Radicalism in thought and religion being taught to the next generation breeds future hate, war, and terror. We must stop being offended and not pass on our offenses to the next generation.

When you recall an offending incident, isn't it often just a minor word, look, or action that doesn't merit continued bitterness. Instead of casting blame on others, look at yourself. How can you take action to reconcile instead of compounding the pain?

So begin to write down the answer to: "What am I angry about?" Then look at it. Is offense and bitterness worth the hurt and separation it has caused? Your body changes when you're mad and when you haven't forgiven. You can see a person physically change. If they are holding on to unforgiveness and the object of their anger walks into the room, you can see their veins start popping out; their breathing gets excessive; they might even start to hyperventilate or their arms may be tightly folded, blocking blessings and blood flow. The physical and spiritual signs are all there—they are offended.

I have asked parents, Is it worth not having your children know their grandmother or their aunt or their cousins because of this offense? So it's about taking the mature step to release the offense and choose forgiveness.

Maturity means taking steps that are not always popular but that are necessary to initiate making *up*.

Frederic Luskin, a PhD in Counseling and Health from Stanford University, has written an insightful book, *Forgive for Good*. His research has demonstrated that forgiveness has been shown to reduce stress, anger, hurt, and depression, while increasing positive feelings such as optimism, hope, compassion, and self-confidence. Remember that what you focus on really shapes your perspective and outlook in life. Dr. Luskin writes,

> Dwelling on wounds gives them power over you. What you remember, or focus your attention on, can be shifted in the same way you change the channel on your TV, if we get used to watching the grievance channel we are likely to see that the world has many grievances, but if we get used to watching the forgiveness channel the world can look very different.[5]

Where you focus is what you picture. Aim a camera, focus, and snap a photograph. Guess what develops? Whatever you focused on became the picture that developed. When you focus on the pain, hurt, and offenses in life, you develop a picture or perspective of life that is filled with unforgiveness and bitterness. Is this the way you really want to see others or how you want them to see you? Choose to forgive. Become a reconciler not a divider. Transform angry destruction into the forgiving construction of new and healthy relationships. Or, if the place where you are prevents you from forgiving, then move on so you can go forward in your spirit. Those whose ancestors were victims of the Holocaust often revisit the places where this crime against humanity took place. It was unforgiveable, and yet we have to find a way to forgive, as Jesus did on the cross, "Father, forgive them, for they know not what they do."

The Virtue of Peacemaking

Peaceful relationships that flow in grace and forgiveness bring blessings to us and those whom we forgive. Inner conflict, which translates into emotional distress, anxiety, worry, and ongoing anger and bitterness, can lead to physical illness as well as relational, emotional, and spiritual brokenness. Consider the reciprocity of peacemaking that results from making up: "Blessed are the peacemakers for they shall be called the sons of God."[6] God's blessing comes upon those who live out reconciliation.

Conflict and misunderstanding seem to mark much of our international relationships as well as our personal encounters. Instead of looking for ways to make up, we constantly find ourselves breaking up marriages, families, and nations. Peacemaking brings wholeness and reconciliation to relationships. How does it work?

Start peacemaking with inner peace. I have discovered that peacemaking begins with inner peace with God. The apostle Paul writes about it this way, "Therefore, since we have been made right in God's sight by faith, *we have peace with God* because of what Jesus Christ our Lord has done for us."[7] Peace with God gives me the inner resources and strength that I need as a wife, mother, pastor, and leader to work for peace in my own relationships and to mediate peace between others in conflict.

Strife often arises from an insistence on getting what we want instead of seeking God's best for others as well as ourselves. I've discovered that conflict is often rooted in my own pride and selfish concerns. I feel I have the right to be treated certain ways and to receive certain things. Truthfully, when I release my personal agendas and self-centered rights, and begin working for the rights of others—the victimized, the weak, the poor, the sick, the imprisoned, and the disenfranchised—I usher peace into my relationships and even relationships among others. Once humility and selflessness dominate my attitude, then peacemaking actions begin in my relationships.

Peacemaking and making up are "about us" not just "about me." So, what characterizes your relationships—conflict or peacemaking? A willingness to make up or break up? I remember in high school during those early dating years how some couples were always fighting and breaking up. Even when they tried to make up, eventually the fighting would start again. They so wanted to be liked or loved, but had no idea how to relate harmoniously and peacefully with others. At the root of their breaking up was always a selfish, insecure attitude of the relationship being "about me" instead of "about us." Over the years, those immature teen attitudes often migrated into and then contaminated marriages. Conflict, separation, and divorce plagued many of the couples I counseled. They refused to learn how to become peacemakers, and so making up wasn't an option and breaking up became the solution—until the next relationship formed and a new war started.

Making up is a choice, a lifestyle. Peacemaking is more than a skill set; it's a lifestyle arising from a compassionate virtue that chooses humility over pride, selflessness over selfishness, forgiveness over offense, and peace over war. Peace isn't the cessation of conflict; it's the decision to work for reconciliation. I invite you to make up with God; decide to proactively work for peace in all your relationships and to become a peacemaker in your family, workplace, and community. Peacemaking seeks win-win solutions so that after the conflict is over the warring parties have experienced healing and reconciliation instead of simply a ceasefire that will soon erupt again into strife. Be a peacemaker. Work for making solutions!

Experiencing Forgiveness in My Family

I have experienced the power of making up in my own family. There was a problem among my siblings that arose around our mother's death. I was totally unprepared for it and surprised at it. I realize now it could have simply been how some people grieved; sometimes when people grieve they take their venom out on somebody else. Well, in this case, I was one of the victims and it was a very painful place to be. The person who hurt me was someone I really, really loved, and it hurt deeply. My way of not being hurt anymore was to not deal with this person at all. I took their number off my cell phone, I took their name off my e-mail and, to make a long story short, I closed the door on this person. Then one day I heard my children saying, "How come we don't see him anymore?" They were growing up, and one of my children was about to graduate. We had been thinking about the people that were significant in their lives, and they started asking about this particular family member.

I had to make a decision as to whether I was going to let my lack of forgiveness rule or whether I was going to take the high road and forgive. I made the decision to invite this person to my child's graduation party. When this person came into the room, we had a three-year-overdue embrace and, even though we had not had an opportunity to talk about our falling out, words were no longer necessary. What is more important is emoting love, the emotional response.

Release the past and the persons who have offended you. Until you make up and release them, you drag the rotting corpses of their offenses with you into all the other relationships of your life. Your unforgiveness of that person contaminates all the other relationships of your life. Make a list of those with whom you need to make up right now. Begin to write, call, e-mail, and visit each one. Forgive. Release. Refuse to take or carry the bait of offense. Jesus said it this way, "Forgive us our trespasses as we forgive those who trespass against us." You've heard it and said it in the Lord's Prayer. Now live it. Make *up!*

Steps to Make *Up*

- Refuse to take the bait of offense.
- Approach those with whom you are offended and reach out to them with forgiveness.
- Release anger and unforgiveness.
- Choose to become a peacemaker.
- Choose to forgive before others repent, and even if they don't repent.
- Focus on forgiveness instead of hurt, anger, and offense.
- Revisit an offense, but then move on in forgiveness.
- Pray out loud the Lord's Prayer and speak the Beatitudes over your life.
- Start *today!*
- Choose one thing you can do today to make up.

CHAPTER 9

Wake Up! ·····························

Wake up, wake up. It's time to start seeing those things you missed along the way—the relationships and the priorities that were important. As I travel and pass through airports, I watch the corporate rush to make a buck and think about the busy businesspeople who rush through life missing their child's graduation, their baby's first word or first step. A recent news article spoke of a public figure who had become so busy that he missed one child's graduation and found out about which college the other child had selected by reading the newspaper. In my opinion, that's just *too* busy. One day we'll wake up and see that a whole life has passed us by. One of my dear friends of thirty-one years died suddenly. I can't tell you how that was a wake-up call for me, her friends, and her family. Friends and family must be an ongoing priority for our time and attention.

You may be working hard to make a living to provide for yourself and your family, but at some point you have to wake up and say, What am I working for? Am I going to miss the people, the places, and the things that I really enjoy because of it? When I get off this boat will I have a family? Will I have anyone to come home to? It's about waking up and saying, What did I miss along the way? What did I do? What are the actions I can take not to miss anymore? There was a famous movie in the seventies, *Lady Sings the Blues,* which had this line, "What good is success if you have no one to share it with?"

It's an up decision to wake up to loving people and using stuff instead of loving stuff and using people.

It's an up decision to wake up to the relationships that are lasting and will be there long after the movers and shakers have left you and gone on to greener pastures.

It's an up decision to wake up to deepening relationships through integrity, honesty, and transparency instead of just superficially connecting with lots of people and then moving on.

It's an up decision to wake up to your long-term, lasting purpose, loving God passionately and people sincerely.

It's an up decision to wake up to seizing each moment of significant opportunity as a gift to maximize for doing good instead of as a right to exploit selfishly for yourself.

I Must Work at Waking Up

I am a speaker and the majority of my income comes from being on the road speaking at conferences, colleges, and conventions. As the mother of two children, I recognize that they need me as well. I made a decision at each of their births that I didn't want somebody else to raise them. To fulfill that vow meant I would have to make some sacrifices in my life. Working at waking up takes time and demands that we make sacrifices.

Waking up means making some personal sacrifices. I wanted to be there for my baby's first steps and when they called out "Daddy" and certainly when they called for "Mommy." To do that meant I had to make some choices about which engagements I could accept. They all were lucrative, and some were really over the top for my personal prestige and profile. Some were on the West Coast and I live on the East Coast. That meant I'd have to fly out there and miss a day on the way out and on the way back. Then I'd have to deal with the jet-lag, and so in a sense I'd lose nearly a week out of my life, and my children's lives. I had to make a decision that I couldn't be on the West Coast, attractive and lucrative as those engagements were at this time in my life. I had to decide what was more important to me, so I made a choice to do mainly Midwest and East Coast engagements, where access to numerous short flights were available and where I could be home before my kids woke up the next morning. Many nights I was still able to tuck them in.

What joy that gave to all of us—to have Mommy tell them their bedtime story. Now they are older and, even as I write today, one of them is on the road with me, seeing what Mommy does, participating in it, and most of all, sharing those precious moments together. Such times are priceless!

Waking up means setting right priorities. Children and family emerged as my top priorities. I wanted to be with my children at the beginning and at the end of their day; I wanted to take them to school and pick them up from school. So that meant I had to choose mainly local engagements, and I had to do some things that were quick and I had to do things during the school day. So I have built my life around my family. I want to have a lasting legacy through my children and children's children— both the natural ones and spiritual ones. Here's some questions I ask when setting a purposeful, important priority:

- Will this make a lasting, even eternal impact or is it simply a momentary, fleeting distraction?
- Is it on-purpose or off-purpose in my pursuit of the highest and best for others and myself?
- Will this deepen the meaningful relationships in

life or simply add draining relationships to my schedule?

- Is this a God-idea or simply a good idea?

Now my life in pastoring is wonderful because we do have the flexibility to build our lives around our family relationships, but I made some decisions so that my profession wouldn't become an obsession. I had to decide how many days I would sleep in my own bed, be home with my children and with my husband. I needed to decide how many of my children's games I would make. I wanted to make all of them. It's amazing because I'm one of the few parents that can come to every game. My kids even say, "Mom, stop yelling out every time you see me," and they give me that little glance because of the peer pressure. But it was that first knowing glance after my shouting for them, when they saw me there, that said "Mom's here," that no one else saw, that no one else heard, that you didn't even have to interpret. I cherish those moments. They are snapshots that create lasting memories in the hearts of children. No honorarium or notice in the newspaper can trump that!

Last year when my oldest son was in the eighth grade he said, "Mom you can't yell out to all the umpires and you can't hug me in front of the guys." So now I have found a creative approach, where he is not embarrassed and I can still get my hug in: I hug all the guys on the team, of course. Now they look for me to hug them and when I haven't gotten around to all of them, they will ask, "Ms. Cook, did you forget something today?" I decided to ask the team, "So you don't want me to call out for you guys anymore?" And they said, "Well, you know, it lets us know somebody is pulling for us, we like it. We really like it." That's one of those moments that let's you know it's worth it.

When my youngest was in preschool, I was doing a lot of traveling. That's when I was with the President's Initiative on Race under President Clinton. I was in two or three cities a day. I remember this one moment that was a wake up for me. First of all, I missed my children while I was on the road. I kept their pictures with me. We didn't have cell phones with pictures yet so I was pulling out my pictures and I was really longing to see them. My maternal feelings were really surfacing. When I finally arrived to pick up my youngest at school on one particular day, he was the last child there. He was just getting ready to cry and one of the teachers looked up and saw me and said, "He just said he really wanted to see his mom." And I burst into tears and said, "And I really wanted to see him too."

It was a wake-up moment. I made a decision that my

son was not going to be spending ten hours a day at a school on a regular basis. There may be once and a while that he might have to do the after school time, but that day when I walked in and he was the last child in the room, that was a wake up for me. I said to myself, No, this is not the life I want for him and certainly not the life I want for me. We needed more connecting and I am going to make sure we get it. One of my friends jokingly asked, "So, what time are you picking up your kids from night school?" I must be on time and there for my children!

Another one of those wake up moments was when my eighth-grader was about to graduate last year. It would be the first significant milestone in his life. His graduation fell right in the middle of a week when I provided leadership as president of Hampton University minister's conference for ten thousand leaders. I could not miss either event. So I hired a car to drive me through the night to my son's graduation since there were no late flights. We rode on treacherous highways in bad weather for eight hours. When we arrived home in New York, it was 6:00 a.m. and my son was still asleep. When he awakened at eight and saw me in my bed and at home for his graduation, he leaped into my arms and exclaimed, "My mom is home!" What a teary moment.

As my sons get older now and want to spend more time with their friends, I am also waking up to my friends, many of whom I could not see so regularly when my children were young and needed my time and attention. So I now have regular, weekly play dates with my friends to catch up on their lives, my life, and current events that have to deal with things other than children. Last week, three of us who had attended a Harvard fellowship program together in 1980 and had not been together since that time, met for teatime at the Ritz Carlton on Central Park South, treated ourselves like royalty, and giggled until it was time for me to pick up my youngest son from school. What a joy. What a treat. What an up!

Cultivate the Virtues of Empathy and Compassion

The ability to empathize with others is at the root of waking up. Notice that I said *empathy,* not sympathy. I am not talking here about feeling sorry or pitying, but rather of a genuine ability to be sensitive to the predicaments and problems of others. It's being softhearted, not hardhearted.

A tsunami of unprovoked tragedy swamps an unprepared, unsuspecting victim. You feel their pain and are moved to reach out with help and love. Compassion is to feel the pathos of others, identify with their suffering, and do whatever you can to wake up the empathy, compassion, and caring help of those around you. Such compassion is embodied in the Christ who reached out to heal the hurting: *And Jesus, when He came out, saw a great multitude and was moved with compassion for them, because they were like sheep not having a shepherd.*[1]

Waking up the suffering and pain of those around us is one form of compassion and empathy. Another manifestation of these virtues is when waking up moves us to take up another's cause and lift them up, using whatever means and resources we have to help. This attitude is well defined by the words of Isaiah, the prophet and priest:

The Spirit of the Sovereign LORD is upon me, because the LORD has appointed me to bring good news to the poor. He has sent me to comfort the brokenhearted and to announce that captives will be released and prisoners will be freed. He has sent me to tell those who mourn that the time of the LORD's favor has come, and with it, the day of God's anger against their enemies. To all who mourn in Israel, he will give beauty for ashes, joy instead of mourning, praise instead of despair. For the LORD has planted them like strong and graceful oaks for his own glory.[2]

Let me unpack this wonderful virtue of waking up with compassion for you that's revealed in this messianic prophecy.

- **Wake up to good news.** Our culture seems to be obsessed with bad news. Ominous, tragic headlines sell magazines and papers. The breaking stories on cable news channels blare out the sirens of school shootings, suicide bombings, mounting death tolls, spreading diseases and plagues, and wars with rumors of more wars. Such bad news desensitizes us and colors our expectations so that we rarely hear or even look for good news. Wake up to the good news that God cares and fills us with the compassion to care for and empathize with others. Wake up to the good news that people still perform random acts of kindness and much good news is interwoven into the fabric of humans created in God's image. Wake up to the good news that you can create good news yourself by demonstrating compassion in small ways that bring smiles and laughter and that ease pain in the lives of those around you. Visit the sick and imprisoned. Volunteer your time in community service. Get equipped to help and counsel people through your house of worship. Feed the hungry. Help the poor and homeless. Mentor or coach a young person trying to find his or her way. Light a candle in the darkness. Be salt and light in the midst of pain and suffering.

- **Afflict the comfortable and comfort the afflicted.** Those who have much often tend to withdraw and smugly ignore the plight of those with little. In a dumb, intentional stupor they walk by the homeless and the beggar on the street. They ignore the abused and disenfranchised. The comfortable become self-righteous believing the grace they have received is a right or deserved instead of a gift. They fail to understand the responsibility to wake up as they have moved up. Compassion becomes a lifestyle when you take others up with you as you move up. Wake up to the ability you have to *write the check*. Embrace a life of giving and investing in others instead of just consuming. In other words, when you cannot go to help the helpless yourself, give generously of your resources to charitable organizations like the Red Cross, Compassion International, Samaritan's Purse, the Salvation Army, your house of worship or church that has demonstrated a compassionate spirit, UNICEF, or any of a host of other organizations that have mobilized people, institutions, and resources to comfort the afflicted.

- **Give beauty for ashes, joy instead of mourning, praise instead of despair.** Find ways to affirm people even in the little things they do right. Instead of judging and condemning, correct and teach with compassion. Choose to discipline by teaching and correcting instead of punishing and crushing. You can make somebody's day with a smile, a kind word, or a generous tip. Slow down, wake up, and lift up others. Waking up isn't a suggestion; it's a divine mandate empowered by the love and compassion of our Creator!

- **Love your enemies.**[3] The way of the world is to defeat, crush, slam, and bomb the enemy. Compassion loves the unlovely and those different from us—in race, religion, gender, nationality, economic status, power, political views, or educational credentials. God is love and those whom God moves up wake up to the reality that God loves our enemies as much as God loves us. Wake up to the need to eradicate from your thinking all notions of prejudice, ethnic superiority, national elitism, or fundamentalist fanaticism that justifies destroying or enslaving others.

Factor in the Familiar

While you are moving up, you must be sensitive to waking up by factoring in the familiar. That's a good delineation or boundary in life. *Factor in the familiar.* You need to factor in what keeps you going.

> *What is it when you're moving up*
> *that you come home to*
> *that keeps you up*
> *and keeps you going?*

The daughters of Zelophehad had discovered that family was more important than tradition, that life the way they had known it within their family was worth fighting for instead of resigning themselves to giving up just because tradition had made no place for their circumstance. They were factoring in the familiar—the family relationships that needed to be preserved.

For me, it's my family, friends, and my faith. During my sabbatical the four of us will be going to church together and I will not be the Reverend Dr. Cook and I won't be called to the pulpit. Sure I'm a worship leader and I'm the preacher, but I'm a wife and mom too, and I want to be with my family singing out of the hymn books together. I don't know how many more years we will all be together. The time will come when my children will be young adults and they will move on with their own families and life dreams.

I don't want to miss the meaning, the common moments of life when being together is more important than anything else I could be doing. So, as I factor in the familiar, I take time for my family. It may mean one less engagement, it may mean three less engagements, it may mean less income. Giving up the immediate for what's lasting means that I have to step back from the demands of the moment and take an objective look at what's happening in my life. Prayer and wise counsel from others help me gain perspective about what's important. I need wisdom, God's perspective, to see the long-term impact of my immediate decisions. I must see the end, the goal, before I start a race. If I am running but going nowhere, then I must take time to wisely step up to a higher perspective in order to understand long-term consequences.

Wake up to where you are going as you run your race of life.

When you celebrate factoring in the familiar, you celebrate the little things in life and discover a new up in your spirit and an inner peace that the turmoil around you cannot disturb. The Scripture says you have a peace that surpasses all understanding. People might not understand how I could give up pastoring or a particular speaking engagement. I have learned that pleasing God with right priorities is so much more important than seeking to please people. I know when I lay down at night what I feel like and I feel up.

In order to wake up so you don't mess up your life and the lives of those closest to you, you may have to give up praise, applause, more money, promotions, or even some things that give you pleasure. Waking up to long-term gain may cause you some short-term pain or sacrifice. Scripture reminds us that trial produces patient perseverance, and patience builds character and this process produces hope that doesn't disappoint, outpouring love from God, and power through the Spirit.[4] The process of waking up may be painful, but it does produce character and maturity.

Don't give up what's important, wake up to it.

Don't rush by the people who are there for you, and remember that you need to be there for them. At a recent very large leadership conference, I had the officers of the conference, stop, sit at a lunch table with the delegates, and refuse to be in a rush mode. The people felt their love and gained even more respect for them as leaders. Wake up.

Don't sacrifice the important and essential for the unimportant, noisy, demanding distractions that are all around you and that will always be there to draw you away from your priorities.

As you move up, wake *up!*

Steps to Wake *Up*

- Factor in the familiar.
- Set priorities in line with your life's purpose, not your immediate demands.
- Seize the God-ideas in life while releasing the plethora of good ideas that keep you busy but accomplish little that's lasting.
- Deepen the close relationships in life, particularly family.
- Take time for what's important; refuse to waste time on draining relationships that have no staying power.
- Be there now and take time with those you will be with throughout life's journey. Begin today. It's not too late to reconnect and recommit.

CHAPTER 10

Cheer Up! --------------------------------

"A cheerful heart is good medicine, but a broken spirit saps a person's strength."[1]

Cheer up is about just doing something fun. It's about laughing, doing something that brings joy to your soul. From prison, St. Paul wrote, "Rejoice in the Lord always, and again I say, rejoice!"[2] Find joy for your soul. Everything in life does not have to be hard. A missionary friend in Belgrade often quoted the ubiquitous proverb, "Life is hard and then you die." Life doesn't have to be that way. Cheer up!

When you move up to a new place some of the journey will be tough, but everything doesn't have to be hard. Often, we make the journey miserable when instead there could be much laughter along the way. Some of the most joyous exchanges in life are the social ones. I'm really basking in them right now. As I write this, I am celebrating twenty-five years in pastoral ministry.

Ministry is filled with ups and downs—but I have chosen to stay up no matter how down the people around me may become. A pastor sees all of life—weddings and funerals; fresh love and broken hearts; healings and terminal illnesses; hirings and firings—it's all there. But in the midst of all of life, we must make time to laugh, to celebrate, to rejoice.

As I approached my fiftieth birthday and my twenty-fifth anniversary of ministry, I told everyone I wanted a real party and people started signing on. I told them there was going to be music and fun. A lot of traditional religious people can't handle events that cheer up life, but my family came from a very social place, full of clean fun. When the family gets together it is fun. Some of the people responded to my party idea with, "We haven't gone out in so long, thank you for creating this fun."

In the Midst of Tragedy, Cheer Up

When 9/11 happened, I was an NYPD chaplain so I had to respond very quickly, immediately, that day. Then afterward we had weeks and months of dealing with death and one of the first things I did when we got through the hardest part was I went straight to a comedy club. We had had so many days of fear and morbidity that I needed laughter and it was medicine for my soul. The Scriptures say forgiveness brings healing, but so does laughter. That's what I need for my soul when I am in anguish. So I find as many places as I possibly can where I can laugh and be cheered up and cheer others as well. There are positive physiological changes that occur within our bodies when we smile and laugh that cause the body to sing.

Take a break and cheer up? You can take a break from the place you are in—and that doesn't mean it has to be an expensive vacation. Take a mini-vacation. It may mean using one of your vacation days and checking into your favorite hotel for a night. For my fiftieth birthday party, we rented out the presidential suite in one of the nearby hotels. First of all, it brought joy to my family. My kids are thrilled any time they can order room service and have company over and they don't have to clean up the place. But it also allowed me to invite some of my closest friends, with whom I had not had a chance to just sit, laugh, and talk with in a long time. And it turned out that that was the last time I would be with one of them. I am so thankful we had those moments together to laugh. My fondest memory was eating chips and salsa with her from the same paper plate, laughing about our thirty-one year friendship.

Take a break and cheer up. In most sporting events, there's what's called a break in the action, a time out. Then the coach calls the players over and commands them to stop, breathe, rest, and be rejuvenated so that they can get back in the game. We need this in the game of life. It may mean going to a park and making a picnic lunch. You need to begin to make a list of things you enjoy doing and then begin to do them. Even if you can't do them all at once or every day you could certainly try them one at a time—take one step at a time.

You know one step at a time. I like sun and water—it's peaceful and soothing. So going to lakes, rivers, and oceans is a way for me to cheer up. I visit a small, unique park here in New York City that is built on the water and that very few people frequent. I can get lost in a city with millions of people. I find that in that place I can quickly cheer up.

Reset and cheer up. You must rest in order to cheer up. Rest is important for renewal. Tired people become crabby, sour people. Like others, I get irritable if I have not had enough rest or sleep. If I'm scolding my children for something that is not really necessary, I step back and think, this is just wrong. Even as I say some sharp remark, I'm thinking to myself, Okay, Miss Haven't Had Enough Sleep Today, what was that all about? Rest up and cheer up.

Go to a place to laugh! I go to comedy clubs. I hang with people who laugh and rejoice with me instead of those who always focus on the sour, dark side of life. I have a couple of people in my life who laugh much, and I make it a point to go to lunch with them or call them up. Take these little steps to cheer up.

Play days. My kids have play days and I have grown-people play days. About once a week I contact a friend and schedule a movie or meet them for breakfast. It's an adult play day. I am really intentional about this because time moves so swiftly. Wouldn't it be sad to get to the end of life and realize you hadn't really lived?

Henry David Thoreau said, "The mass of men lead lives of quiet desperation and go to their grave with their song still in them." I want my song to come out, my purpose to be fulfilled, and my laughter to infect all those around me.

Don't overload yourself. Cheering up also means I'm not putting too much on my plate. It's being with people and in places that I want to be. It's playing. And it also means taking some things off your plate that don't need to be there. When you start a diet, one of the first techniques is to cut your portions in half to see immediate results. For immediate results with your spiritual diet, cut your workload in half. One of my dear friends said to me when I began pastoring and was complaining of being run-down, "Cut your counseling load in half." That one simple step, I am convinced, saved my life. Overloaded planes can't fly. Overloaded people fail.

Cheering up can be playing a sport that you like. For me it's basketball; for some it's rollerblading. For others it's getting on a swing. I starting swinging on a park swing the other day. I can't remember when I was last on a swing. Can you? You know what? My whole countenance changed just from swinging high on that swing. I recently started swimming in the mornings in an indoor pool. My entire being is lifted with each completed lap. Stress is alleviated with every stroke. My days begin quite differently now.

The daughters of Zelophehad were not moved by anger. I think anger would have canceled their blessing. Give and it shall be given to you.[3] Walk in the way you want to be treated and get creative. Find a positive way to approach a negative person. Find the joy in something miserable. Laugh with others and laugh at yourself.

Find the approach that will work in your context. With the listening up, you'll learn your context; you'll know who's who and who to speak to and who not to speak to in terms of your request. Is it time to ask for a raise? Timing is everything. Is it time for someone to speak on your behalf? Is this the day, or has the supervisor just gotten a bad report and this is not the day? Put on a smile. Laugh. Cheer up.

So it's all about making decisions out of joy instead of anger that end up in tune with your life and with your flow and with your God. Is your head hanging down with sorrow and burdens? Look up to God. He can cheer you up by lifting you up.

> *But You, O LORD, are a shield for me,*
> *My glory and the One who lifts up my head.*[4]

The other thing the daughters of Zelophehad did was that they faced up. They faced up to a society that had been closed to them. By their very presence and their very willingness to take a stand, the law was changed, and it revolutionized their society. The Lord said something like this to Moses, "Yes, what the daughters of Zelophehad said is true. It is correct. So anytime somebody comes to you, whether a son or a daughter, and their parents have died, you give them their inheritance. You don't have to come back to Me it's settled."[5]

They chose to face up to the culture, to be positive instead of negative, to move up instead of down, to cheer up instead of going around like a group of victims bemoaning their fate. You have choice. Deuteronomy says "Choose life." Life means cheering up even when faced with death or dreadful or challenging situations.

Embrace the Virtue of Joy

Cheering up is a choice, not a response. If our joy is simply happiness—responding to pleasant circumstances that happen our way—then we will certainly experience things that will rob our joy and make us unhappy. But I can choose to be joyful even in the midst of pain and suffering. Consider this paradoxical directive: "Consider it pure joy, my brothers, whenever you face trials of many kinds."[6]

Joy comes from within. It's an inner decision to look up and cheer up even when everything and everyone around us is looking down and pulling others down with them. Joy isn't frivolous; it's a confidence that while something may knock me down, nothing can keep me down. I know who and whose I am—that gives me a joy that no one and nothing can rob. I like the way Jesus described such joy: "These things I have spoken to you, that in Me you may have peace. In the world you will have tribulation; but be of good cheer, I have overcome the world."[7]

James Taylor croons his familiar rendition of the song

"You've Got a Friend." That's part of the secret of inner joy: It's knowing you're not alone. A Friend above and friends around you will see you through the storm to the next sunrise knowing that "those who sow in tears shall reap in joy."[8] It's true that no one can promise you a rose garden, but inner joy will always overcome the thorns of life. Identify your source of joy. Fill up through laughter, singing, friendship, giving, and moments of refreshing. Tap into the limitless joy that comes from befriending God. Make this your declaration before the living God:

> *You will show me the path of life;*
> *In Your presence is fullness of joy;*
> *At Your right hand are pleasures forevermore.*[9]

Move Up by Cheering Up

Who or what is pulling you down? Resist the downward momentum. Choose to move up by cheering up. Laugh. Find the humor in situations. Laugh at the enemy, the attack, and the troubles. Laughter will lighten your countenance and give you another perspective for facing up to reality. Cheer *up!*

Steps to Cheer *Up*

- Take a break in the action. You may be too tired to laugh.

- Find people who will laugh with you, not at you.

- Associate with people who cheer you up instead of tear you down.

- Choose to respond with joy; reject the myth that others or things can *make you happy*.

- Identify a place that you can go to, be interested in, and be cheered up.

- Laugh at yourself. Don't be so serious and stodgy.

- Think up ways to cheer up others; by giving cheer you will receive cheer!

- Schedule a play day or fun day for yourself.

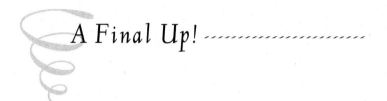

A Final Up! ----------------------------------

just know it. You're sitting there thinking, "I can think of other *ups* that you missed!" Of course you can, so can I. That's wonderful. Start thinking, creating, and discovering more ways to move up in life. Don't just sit there; get up! Start up! Declare I'm moving up!—TODAY!

I can help you start up imagining some other ups for living a blessed life:

- **Move up**. This up permeates all the others. What decisions and actions do you need to implement now to move up in the future? Procrastination will always keep you in a rut when you need to move up. What have you been putting off? Getting your GED, diploma, license, or degree? Taking that continuing education you need? Investing your time or your money in something that will take you or others to the next level? Making that apology or forgiving that offensive person? Reaching out to help others in need?

- **Get up**. Stop being comfortable, lazy, and complacent. You will never stand up until you first decide to get up.
- **Start up**. Battery dead? Out of gas? Need rest, refreshing, or renewing? Is there a vacation, sabbatical, or simply a day off that you need to take?
- **Shape up**. I'm talking about eating right, exercising, and taking care of your body—a gift from God. You can only move up when you shape up!
- **Reach up**. Somebody at the next level is where you want to be. You don't have to put them down or step on them to move up. Ask for their help. Seek out their mentoring, teaching, or coaching.
- **Shut up**. Momma used to tell me not to say that to others, but at times, I need to say it to myself. As long as I am aimlessly chattering, I will never hear what God or others are trying to say to me.
- **Build up**. Take time to refresh, renew, and be built up by events and others who can impart meaning into your life. Take time to build up others instead of tearing them down.
- **Wise up**. Wisdom takes the long look and gets God's perspective on the matter. Wisdom, knowledge, and understanding all work together empowering you to make wise and right decisions in life.

- **Measure up**. Examine the myths and prejudices you have been raised with or taught by your culture. Measure what you think and believe against the truth of God's revelation in Scripture, which has stood the test of time.
- **Go up**. Go up to the next level in your life skills, educational preparation, job training, and spiritual maturity.
- **Hook up**. Connect with positive, creative, affirming, and supportive people who are moving up themselves and who will encourage you as well.
- **Grow up**. Set aside childish, immature emotions and beliefs. I like these biblical words: "When I was a child, I spoke and thought and reasoned as a child does. But when I grew up, I put away childish things."[1]
- **Keep up**. Keep up and keep pace with the times. Don't be frustrated by falling behind, looking bad, and continually wanting the good ol' days that are done and gone.

Permit me to suggest a brief homework assignment for your consideration. Now, don't moan and groan as my children would do. Simply check off the *ups* you know you need to work on, starting now:

- ☐ Stand Up
- ☐ Speak Up
- ☐ Look Up
- ☐ Book Up
- ☐ Kiss Up
- ☐ Listen Up
- ☐ Hang Up
- ☐ Make Up
- ☐ Wake Up
- ☐ Cheer Up

Set some goals and timelines for yourself. Decide that you will move up to a new level instead of rocking along and remaining comfortable and complacent where you are right now. *Up* is a choice, not a command, and it is certainly not something that will just happen. *Up* takes time, effort, attentiveness, and commitment! Identify people around you who seem to specialize in an *up* in which you need improvement and growth. Let them mentor or coach you. Hang with them. Ask questions. Imitate them. Develop a hunger and thirst for moving up.

I came back from a trip the other day and my car had been parked outside the whole time I was gone. I put my key in the ignition like always, turned the key, and nothing happened at first. It took a little cranking before it would start. The car was used to movement but it had been outside unused and so it was not ready to move after sitting for so long. But when I settled myself and I settled it and I turned the key again, it was ready to *start up.*

All of the ups in this book will never happen until you get up and start up. You may have been idling and have been in an environment with all kinds of elements coming at you, but try this thing and put the key in again. It's time to start up, rev up, and go to a new place. So come on, when racecar drivers have been sitting awhile they hear the words, "Start your engines." This, too, is directed to you.

So don't be frustrated with what hasn't happened in the past. The past is over; get up and start up. Go out and buy copies of this book for your friends. Give it to them. Help them *up! My logo for my company says, Lifting Lives to New Levels. In other words, this book can help lift them up.*

Now, you there, get up. The great highway of life awaits you. There's a new part of the highway that has been built that you have not discovered. There was an Exit 1 before, but this is a new Exit 1. And if you're willing to start up your car and travel on this new road, there are things you will discover about yourself and about the new places that God is taking you. He will take you places that you have never been.

It will be an exciting journey for you. Your engine has already been filled up for you. God has just been waiting for you to say you're ready to go up. When you're ready, God's ready. Let's go forward. Get up. Start *up!*

Notes

Biblical quotations are from the King James Version unless otherwise noted.

Introduction

1. Ronald F. Youngblood, ed., *Nelson's Illustrated Bible Dictionary* (Nashville: Thomas Nelson Publishers, 1986).
2. Numbers 27:1–11.
3. Isaiah 40:31 (New King James Version).
4. Job 13:15 (NKJV).
5. Read Daniel 6.
6. Martin Luther King Jr., *Strength to Love* (New York: Pocket Books, 1964).
7. Psalms 121:1–2 (New Living Translation).
8. Luke 1:37.

1. Stand Up!

1. John 5:8 (NLT) (emphasis added).
2. Proverbs 23:7.

3.   Ephesians 6:13–14.

4.   Acts 14:9–10.

5.   Psalms 139:14.

6.   Jeremiah 18:1–4 (NLT).

7.   Psalms 27:14 (NKJV).

8.   Amos 5:24.

9.   Joshua 1:9 (New International Version).

2. *Speak Up!*

1.   Ecclesiastes 37b (NLT).

2.   1 Peter 2:10 (The Living Bible).

3.   Psalms 68:6.

4.   James 1:17; Jeremiah 29:11–12 (NLT).

5.   Romans 8:28 (NIV).

6.   Read 2 Timothy 1:7.

7.   Proverbs 18:16.

8.   Matthew 26:11.

9.   Acts 4:13 (NKJV).

10. Philippians 1:20.

11. Galatians 1:10 (NKJV).

12. John 8:32.

13. John L. Mason, *An Enemy Called Average.*

14. Catherine Day, *Shared Heart Journal* (Writers Club Press, 2002), p. 107.

3. Look Up!

1. Amos 5:4.

2. Psalms 121:1–2.

3. See Exodus 33.

4. Psalms 139:1–10 (NLT).

5. Psalms 24:1–2.

6. Deuteronomy 31:6; Hebrews 13:5.

7. Psalms 71:5.

8. 2 Corinthians 4:6–9 (NLT).

9. 2 Timothy 2:15 (KJV).

10. Pastor Hezekiah Walker, *Family Affair II: Live at Radio City Music Hall* (New York, NY: Verity, 2002).

11. Joshua 1.

12. Psalms 46:10.

13. 2 Corinthians 5:17.

4. Book Up!

1. 1 Chronicles 4:10 (NKJV).

2. http://en.wikipedia.org/wiki/List_of_best-selling-books.

5. Kiss Up!

1. Ephesians 4:32.

2. Jeremiah 29:11–13 (NIV).

3. Matthew 7:1.

4. Matthew 5:1–10 (NLT).

5.   Mark 4.

6.   Romans 12:1–2 (NKJV).

7.   http://www.drsujay.com/store.html.

8.   1 Chronicles 4:9 (NKJV).

9.   Philippians 2:5–11.

10.   Luke 16:9–10 (NLT).

6. Listen Up!

1.   Ecclesiastes 3:1–8.

2.   1 Kings 19:11–13 (NIV).

3.   Acts 17:28.

4.   Psalms 119:105.

5.   Romans 15:7.

6.   Ephesians 4:15.

7.   "In the Garden," words and music by Charles Austin Miles, 1913.

8.   John 16:1–15.

7. Hang Up!

1.   Isaiah 43:18–19.

2.   John 5:1–15.

3.   Proverbs 11:14.

4.   Read John 14–16.

5.   Jeremiah 29:11–12 (NIV).

6.   Larry Bossidy, Ram Charan, and Charles Burck,

Execution: The Discipline of Getting Things Done (New
York: Crown Business, 2002), p. 19.

7. Psalms 1:1–3.

8. 1 Chronicles 12:32 (NLT).

8. Make Up!

1. James 1:19.

2. Luke 17:1–4.

3. John Brevere, *The Bait of Satan* (Lake Mary: Charisma
    House, 1994), p. 5.

4. Ephesians 4:26.

5. Frederic Luskin, *Forgive for Good* (New York: Harper
    Collins, 2002), p. 10.

6. Matthew 5:9 (NKJV).

7. Romans 5:1 (NLT) (emphasis added).

9. Wake Up!

1. Mark 6:34 (NKJV).

2. Isaiah 61:1–4 (NLT).

3. Matthew 5:44.

4. Read Romans 5.

10. Cheer Up!

1. Proverbs 17:22 (NLT).

2. Philippians 4:4 (NKJV).

3. Luke 6:38 (NKJV).

4.   Psalms 3:3 (NKJV).

5.   Paraphrase of Numbers 27:5–11.

6.   James 1:2 (NIV).

7.   John 16:33 (NKJV).

8.   Psalms 126:5 (NKJV).

9.   Psalms 17:11.

A Final Up!

1.   1 Corinthians 13:11 (NLT).

About the Author

Dr. Suzan Johnson Cook, better known as Dr. Sujay, is an inspirational life coach, mentor, and motivator who resides in New York City. Described by the *New York Times* as "Oprah and Billy Graham" rolled into one, she is known for her motivational tools that help people to advance their lives, maximize their potential, "look up and move up." On the frontlines at Harvard, Harlem, and 9/11, she has been a dynamic leader on the local and national political fronts. She has appeared on numerous television programs and will soon debut her own talk show. Her previous bestselling book is *Live Like You're Blessed*. Dr. Sujay is the executive director of the Moving Up Institute and is widely known for her Wonderful Wall Street™ Wednesdays, standing-room-only lunchtime seminars and services for the Wall Street community. She has given more than a thousand speeches.